# MAHESH CHAVDA

## God's Miraculous Power

### WORD PUBLISHING

Word (UK) Ltd
Milton Keynes, England

WORD AUSTRALIA
Kilsyth, Victoria, Australia

WORD COMMUNICATIONS LTD
Vancouver, B.C., Canada

STRUIK CHRISTIAN BOOKS (PTY) LTD
Maitland, South Africa

CHRISTIAN MARKETING NEW ZEALAND LTD
Havelock North, New Zealand

JENSCO LTD
Hong Kong

JOINT DISTRIBUTORS SINGAPORE –
ALBY COMMERCIAL ENTERPRISES PTE LTD
and
CAMPUS CRUSADE
SALVATION BOOK CENTRE
Malaysia

ISBN 0-85009-804-1 (Australia 1-86258-254-8)

Unless otherwise indicated, Scripture quotations are from the New International Version (NIV), © 1973, 1978, 1984 by International Bible Society.
Other Scripture quotations are from the following sources:
The New American Standard Bible (NASB), © 1960, 1962, 1963, 1968, 1971, 1972, 1973, 1975, 1977 the Lockman Foundation.
The Authorised Version of the Bible (AV).

The quotations in the following studies are all used by permission.

**Study 1** from *Amazing Love*, by Graham Kendrick, © 1989, Make Way Music, P.O. Box 683, Hailsham, East Sussex, BN27 4ZB.
**Study 2** from *Destined for the Throne*, by Paul E. Billheimer, © 1975 Christian Literature Crusade.
**Study 3** from *Who by Faith*, by R. T. Kendall, © 1981 by R. T. Kendall. Hodder & Stoughton Ltd.
**Study 5** from *The Imitation of Christ*, by Thomas à Kempis, translated by Leo Sherley-Price (Penguin Classics, 1952), translation copyright © Leo Sherley-Price 1952.
**Study 6** from *Men of Destiny*, by Terry Virgo, © Terry Virgo 1987. Kingsway Publications.
**Study 7** from *The Normal Christian Life*, by Watchman Nee, © 1961 Angus I. Kinnear. Kingsway Publications.
**Studies 8, 26** from *The Weapons of Your Warfare*, by Larry Lea, © 1984 by Larry Lea. Word (UK) Ltd.
**Studies 9, 12, 25** from *Know the Truth*, by Bruce Milne, © Bruce Milne 1982. IVP.
**Study 11** from *The Preacher's Portrait*, by John Stott, © Copyright Wm. B. Eerdmans Publishing Co. 1961. Wm. B. Eerdmans Publishing Co., 255 Jefferson Ave S.E., Grand Rapids, Michigan 49503.
**Studies 13, 14** from *Prayer: Key to Revival*, by Paul Y. Cho, © 1984 by Word Incorporated. Word (UK) Ltd.
**Study 15** from *Celebration of Discipline*, by Richard J. Foster, © 1978 by Richard J. Foster. Hodder & Stoughton Ltd., Sevenoaks, Kent/USA, Philippines and Canada, HarperCollinsPublishers Inc.
**Studies 16, 24, 31** from *The Positive Kingdom*, by Colin Urquhart, © 1985 by Colin Urquhart. Hodder & Stoughton Ltd.
**Study 17** from *Can You Hear the Heartbeat?* by Dave Andrews, © 1989 by Dave Andrews and David Engwicht. Hodder & Stoughton Ltd.
**Study 18** from *Only Love Can Make a Miracle*, by Mahesh Chavda, © 1990 by Mahesh Chavda. Kingsway Publications/USA Servant Publications, Box 8617, Ann Arbor, Michigan 48107.
**Study 19** from *Power Healing*, by John Wimber, © 1986 by John Wimber and Kevin Springer. Hodder & Stoughton Ltd.
**Study 20** from *Freedom to Choose*, by Ernest Gruen, © 1976 by Whitaker House. Whitaker House, 580 Pittsburgh Street, Springdale, PA 15144.
**Study 21** from *I Believe in Satan's Downfall*, by Michael Green, © 1981 by Michael Green. Hodder & Stoughton Ltd.
**Study 22** from *Jesus is the Answer*, by Andrae Crouch, © Copyright 1972 by Lexicon Music. Text reproduced by permission of Boosey & Hawkes Music Publishers Ltd.
**Study 23** from *Miracle Power*, by Jamie Buckingham, © Jamie Buckingham 1988. (Published in Britain) Kingsway Publications/(Published in America) Servant Publications.
**Study 27** from *Spiritual Depression*, by Martyn Lloyd-Jones, © 1965 D. Martyn Lloyd-Jones. Published by Marshall Pickering, an imprint of HarperCollinsPublishers Ltd./USA Eerdmans.
**Study 28** from *Joy Unspeakable*, by Martyn Lloyd-Jones, © Bethan Lloyd-Jones 1984. Kingsway Publications.
**Study 29** from *Power Evangelism*, by John Wimber, © 1985 by John Wimber and Kevin Springer. Hodder & Stoughton Ltd./USA and Philippines, HarperCollinsPublishers Inc.
**Study 30** from *Issues Facing Christians Today*, by John Stott, © by John Stott 1984 and 1990. Published by Marshall Pickering, an imprint of HarperCollinsPublishers Ltd./USA IVP.

*Created and designed by* Frontier Publishing International, BN3 4EH, England
*Reproduced, printed and bound in Great Britain for* Word (UK) Ltd. *by* BPCC Hazells Ltd., member of BPCC Ltd.

93 94 95 96 / 10 9 8 7 6 5 4 3 2 1

# Making the most of the studies ...

Welcome

Welcome to the Oasis study on *God's Miraculous Power*! In this book, Mahesh Chavda explains that the gospel of the Kingdom is not just about words, but about wonders too. He relates some of the marvellous miracles and works of God that he has seen and encourages us to begin reaching out to others in the power of the Spirit.

2 days equals 2 months

We suggest you take two days to go through each study and therefore two months to complete the book. You might want to cover the material more quickly, but if you take your time you are likely to benefit more. We recommend that you use the New International Version of the Bible (post-1983 version). The important thing is not that you finish fast, but that you hear from God *en route*! So aim to learn well and steadily build the teaching into your life.

Move's it in power

Jesus said, 'As the Father has sent me, I am sending you' (John 20:21b). Mahesh looks at this verse and reasons that Christians who have the same anointing as Jesus should be doing exactly the same things as He did.

Mahesh stresses the power of the Word of God to deliver people from sin, sickness and demon oppression. He encourages us to walk in the Spirit and to have a deep compassion — particularly for the poor. He also deals with subjects like our great value to God, baptism in the Spirit, the blood of Christ and fasting. The miracles that he witnesses are truly remarkable, but he consistently gives all the glory to Jesus.

The three sections under the main text relate to the teaching material. You may be asked to think about a particular issue, answer a question, or simply to do something practical. The questions and Scripture verses have been designed to challenge you to move out in greater power.

Build a storehouse

The Bible says, 'Wise men store up knowledge' (Prov. 10:14), and Jesus underlines this when He calls us to '[bring] good things out of the good stored up in [our] heart' (Luke 6:45).

The 'Food for thought' section will give you the invaluable opportunity of hearing from God direct and of storing up all that He says to you. **Please use a separate notebook** particularly for this section. Not only will it help you to crystallise your own thoughts, but it will also be of tremendous reference value in the future.

As you study, refuse to let time pressurise you. Pray that God will speak to you personally and expect Him to do so. You may sometimes find that you are so enthralled by what He says to you that you are looking up many Scriptures which are not even suggested!

Finally, may God bless you as you work your way through this book. As you read, may He give you faith to believe Him for many mighty things. And may He stir you to reach out to those who need to know the love and power of Jesus Christ.

# Jesus' treasure

'What good will it be for a man if he gains the whole world, yet forfeits his soul? Or what can a man give in exchange for his soul?'
(Matt. 16:26)

'The kingdom of heaven is like treasure hidden in a field. When a man found it, he hid it again, and then in his joy went and sold all he had and bought that field' (Matt. 13:44).

T he lead story in an issue of *Time* magazine concerned a fabulously wealthy man. As I read it I thought, 'He looks like the richest person alive, but he's not. The richest people are those who have seen the Kingdom of God.'

If you asked Jesus, 'Which is of greater value to you: all the riches in the world or one soul?' He would point to the soul and say, 'That's worth far more to me than anything else.' Jesus wants you to know how important you are to Him. Such knowledge comes only by revelation but once you've received it, it will change your life and transform your ministry.

An unusual interpretation of the parable of the treasure in the field will give us some idea of Jesus' love for us. Consider the man as Jesus, the field as the world and the treasure as God's people. Now when the man finds the treasure, he doesn't immediately tell everyone about it because he knows that if others realise its worth, they will all want it. Instead, he hides the treasure and decides to purchase the field. Maybe people ask him, 'Why do you want the field? It's worthless — nothing grows in it and it's full of weeds and brambles.' But the man knows that the field contains something of

## ■ To consider

It is easy to think that God loves others but not me — I'm not worthy of His love.

The fact is that none of us is worthy but Jesus died for each and every one of us even though we were sinners. We have not earned our salvation — it is by the grace of God that we have been saved.

## ■ To meditate on

Think about God's love for you.
'But because of his great love for us, God, who is rich in mercy, made us alive with Christ even when we were dead in transgressions' (Eph. 2:4,5).
'It was not with perishable things such as silver or gold that you were redeemed ... but with the precious blood of Christ, a lamb without blemish or defect' (1 Pet. 1:18,19).

infinite value. That's why he joyfully sells all that he has to buy it.

We read that 'God so loved the world that he gave his one and only Son, that whoever believes in him shall not perish but have eternal life' (John 3:16). Jesus knew that not everyone would believe in Him, but He paid for the world because He saw the treasure hidden in it. What was that treasure? A great company of 'whoevers'. This wonderful truth appears again in Titus 2:14 where we read that Jesus 'gave himself for us to redeem us from all wickedness and to purify for himself a people that are his very own'. If you are a Christian, you are part of Jesus' treasure. He has bought you, so you belong to Him.

If treasure lies underground for some time, it will be tarnished by the mud. That's why God has given us the ministries of apostle, prophet, evangelist, pastor and teacher. These servants are given the task of finding the treasure, unearthing it and cleaning it until it shines. In other words, they 'prepare God's people for works of service' (Eph. 4:12). God wants each of us to see how precious we are to Him and to live for His glory.

➢ Look at Paul's prayer for the Ephesian church (Eph. 3:14–21). Notice the progression in the prayer.

➢ What does Paul ask for first? What do they need power for? What does knowing the love of God lead to?

➢ Meditate on each stage of this prayer and then make it your own.

■ **To pray**

Pray for a greater revelation of God's love for you.

Ask the Lord to show you how much He loves you as an individual.

Thank God for His love.

**Amazing love**
**Oh what sacrifice**
**The Son of God giv'n for**
**me**
**My debt He pays and my**
**death He dies**
**That I might live.**
*Graham Kendrick*
*'Amazing Love'*

# A pearl of great value

'The kingdom of heaven is like a merchant looking for fine pearls. When he found one of great value, he went away and sold everything he had and bought it' (Matt. 13:45,46).

The parable of the treasure in the field is accompanied by another parable — about a pearl of great value. Again, I like to see the central character as Jesus who is a merchant in search of fine pearls. When he finds the one that he wants, he doesn't quibble about the price with the seller because he knows how precious it is. Instead, he sells everything and buys it.

Wherever I travel I come across one common problem: people feel worthless. The devil has trampled all over their self-esteem and they've come to the conclusion, 'I really don't matter.' It's a lie! Jesus wouldn't leave heaven's riches and sacrifice His life for something worthless. You're infinitely precious to Him. Your life has value. He loves you.

A while ago I was conducting a crusade in Costa Rica and at the end of the meeting hundreds came forward for prayer. Among them was a large Spanish woman in her late fifties who was evidently very poor as she was wearing frayed tennis shoes and torn clothing. When I reached her I put my hand on her head and she took hold of it and placed it right above her breast. At first, I was embarrassed, then I realised that in that spot she had a tumour the

## ■ To appreciate

Read Philippians 2:6,7.
How did Jesus limit Himself when He came to earth?

_____

_____

_____

Do you have a similar attitude?

## ■ To meditate on

Remember what Jesus has done for you.
'(Jesus) made himself nothing ... he humbled himself and became obedient to death — even death on a cross!' (Phil. 2:7,8)
'He was delivered over to death for our sins and was raised to life for our justification' (Rom. 4:25).

size of a grapefruit. She told my interpreter that it was malignant and that, humanly speaking, there was no hope. She stood there, tears streaming down her face, crying out to Jesus. I was filled with compassion for her. 'Lord, she's one of your precious people,' I thought. 'You gave everything for her.' Then I moved on and prayed for others in the line.

A few moments later my interpreter nudged me and pointed to the platform. Standing up there was the Spanish lady. She was telling everyone, 'I had a malignant tumour and now it's completely disappeared.' She was glorifying Jesus. It was wonderful.

I've ministered to many different types of people. I remember a paralytic boy who smelt terrible, and a poor leper. I held them in my arms and said, 'Jesus loves you. Jesus loves you.' As I did so I felt the joy of the Holy Spirit. He was saying, 'I'd rather be here with these precious ones than anywhere else.' Some might think, 'Do they really matter?' Yes, they do. They're as precious to Jesus as that pearl was to the merchant. Let God fill you with a new compassion for the ones that others would consider 'worthless'. Jesus died for them.

## ■ Food for thought

> Read Mark 10:45; Romans 3:24; Galatians 4:4,5; Ephesians 1:7; Titus 2:14.

> What do you understand by the word 'redemption'?

> Write out your own definition.

_____

_____

_____

_____

## ■ To challenge

What is your attitude to the poor and needy?

Do you express love to them or do you walk by like the priest and the Levite in the story of the Good Samaritan?

Repent of any wrong attitudes you have been holding and ask God to help you see others as He sees them.

**All that have been or ever will be born from the dawn of human history to the dawn of eternal ages are included in God's all embracing redemptive love.**
*Paul E. Billheimer*

# He refused

By faith Moses, when he had grown up, refused to be known as the son of Pharaoh's daughter. He chose to be ill-treated along with the people of God rather than to enjoy the pleasures of sin for a short time. He regarded disgrace for the sake of Christ as of greater value than the treasures of Egypt, because he was looking ahead to his reward (Heb. 11:24–26).

An Egyptian Pharaoh had unimaginable power and authority, magnificence and wealth. You trembled before him and if you sneezed at the wrong moment you would probably lose your head.

Moses was brought up in this atmosphere. He was called 'the son of Pharaoh's daughter' and was educated 'in all the wisdom of the Egyptians and was powerful in speech and action' (Acts 7:22). He could have had all the prestige he wanted. But he rejected it and identified with the people of God instead.

Christians are called to make clear choices. False gods are worshipped as much now as they were in Moses' time. They aren't the gods of the Nile, the crocodile and the fish, but of science, wealth and drugs. I once read about a man who was in a pop group which was making about a million dollars a week. He had everything: cars, women, drugs — and in the end he killed himself.

A young woman came up for prayer at one of my healing meetings. She was carrying a baby. When I asked her how I could pray for her, she began sobbing. She told me that she'd been married for a year and had given AIDS to her

## ■ To beware

We must not have a foot in both camps. We need to refuse anything which entices us away from following the Lord wholeheartedly.

Is there anything in your life which you need to refuse?

Write down in a notebook any action you need to take.

## ■ To meditate on

We need to deal with sin in our lives.
'You may be sure that your sin will find you out' (Num. 32:23b).
'For the wages of sin is death' (Rom. 6:23a).
'All wrongdoing is sin' (1 John 5:17a).

husband. Then she said, 'Our baby has it now and all three of us are dying.' A few years previously someone had offered her drugs. The fun was short-lived. Now she was suffering the consequences of that momentary 'high'.

Satan loves to conceal the end result by focusing on the temporary pleasure that sin usually brings. 'You want nice things?' he says. 'Well I'll give them to you. If you're not satisfied with a Mercedes, have a Rolls Royce — or even three. How about some designer clothes too? And you really must experiment with sex and narcotics.'

While Satan offers you anything you want in this life, the Holy Spirit whispers, 'I may not give you earthly riches and make you into a Hollywood star, but I will give you peace, joy and eternal life. And one day you'll have a glorified body and will rule over angels.'

Moses could have been known as 'the son of Pharaoh's daughter' (Heb. 11:24b) and have all the benefits that went with it, but he chose to suffer with God's people. Why? Because he was looking ahead to his reward. The way you choose will reveal whether you're living for this world or the next.

➤ Read Mark 10:17–22.

➤ Compare the rich young man with Moses. What did Jesus ask him to 'refuse'? Why do you think he was so reluctant? Do you think he understood what was at stake for him?

➤ What is the importance of 'refusing'?

## ■ To consider

Paul considers everything a loss compared to knowing Jesus (Phil. 3:7–11).

Look up some Scriptures on the rewards God gives His people, e.g. Mark 10:30; Col. 3:23,24.

It is not the fool who esteems the reproach of Christ more valuable than the treasures and pleasures of this life. It is the fool who doesn't.
*R. T. Kendall*

# He chose

He withdrew about a stone's throw beyond them, knelt down and prayed, 'Father, if you are willing, take this cup from me; yet not my will, but yours be done' (Luke 22:41,42).

I n the Garden of Gethsemane Jesus could easily have refused to take the world's sin and sicknesses on His shoulders. But the Holy Spirit was with Him, urging Him to complete the work that He had begun. When Jesus eventually got up, He had made His choice — He would be God's instrument of salvation and fulfil His plan for the nations.

We can't choose to be 'the son of Pharaoh's daughter' and at the same time be instruments of salvation. The Spirit urges us to refuse our own way, but He also makes clear that such a choice will be costly. If you're going to be bold for Christ, spiritual forces will oppose you and people will persecute you. You must be prepared for it, and you must stand firm in the power of the Holy Spirit if you're going to accomplish the task that God has given you.

Moses discovered the way through: he 'saw him who is invisible' (Heb. 11:27b). He said to himself, 'I don't want all that wealth and honour if it keeps me from worshipping the God of my fathers.' Later the Lord spoke to Moses from the burning bush and commissioned him to deliver the Israelites from their bondage. When Moses asked Him for His name, He

## ■ To reflect

God chooses the weak and the lowly to accomplish His purposes.

Our boast should be not in ourselves but in the Lord who equips us to do His work.

## ■ To meditate on

Choosing to follow the Lord is costly. 'If anyone would come after me, he must deny himself and take up his cross and follow me' (Matt. 16:24b). 'Those who belong to Christ Jesus have crucified the sinful nature with its passions and desires' (Gal. 5:24).

replied, 'I AM WHO I AM' (Exod. 3:14a). God is the same today as He was in the time of Moses.

When I became a Christian I went to an evangelical church and was fanatical about Jesus. The people there looked at me and said, 'You'll come down to earth' and I wondered if there was something wrong with me. But the problem was with them. They were worshipping not the great 'I am' but the great 'I was'.

Today God looks down on the poor and oppressed and says, 'I've seen the misery of those destroyed by drugs or alcohol; I've watched the desperate plight of the homeless; I've heard the cries of the little children who are being abused by their relatives, and I'm sending you. Tell them that the great "I am" has sent you to them.'

Like Moses, you may protest, 'But who am I? I can't speak. What can I do?' Take your eyes away from yourself and see the One who is invisible. He will anoint you to do amazing things, but first there has to be a refusing and a choosing. Give yourself to God's purposes. Pay the price. Some day you will meet the One who made the ultimate sacrifice for you. And you will agree with Him, 'It was worth it.'

■ **Food for thought**

➤ Read Ephesians 6:10–17.

➤ Write down in a notebook how each part of the armour of God can help you to stand firm.

➤ Are you wearing the armour of God?

■ **To choose**

Spend time considering what the Lord has called you to. Think about what it will cost you.

Write down your commitment to follow the Lord.

_____

_____

**Only those who see the invisible can do the impossible.**
*Anon*

# The stripping process

Naaman was ... a valiant soldier, but he had leprosy ... Elisha sent a messenger to say to him, 'Go, wash yourself seven times in the Jordan, and your flesh will be restored and you will be cleansed.' But Naaman went away angry ... Naaman's servants went to him and said, 'My father, if the prophet had told you to do some great thing, would you not have done it? How much more, then, when he tells you, "Wash and be cleansed"?'
(2 Kings 5:1,10–13)

I wonder how Naaman's servants reacted as they watched their master take off his fine clothes. When he was stripped to the waist they would no longer see him as the great victorious general but as a simple man with a need.

God wanted to do more than heal Naaman. He wanted him to humble himself. For years he had hidden his leprosy, but now the layers of protective clothing were gone. He was exposed to the world. It hurt his pride, but when he came out of the water, he was a changed man.

The Lord loves to touch people with a need, but He often works in ways that we don't like. We come to Him with all our layers and He humbles us. Like Naaman, we think, 'Is this stripping process necessary?' and we wonder how much more we can take.

I remember one occasion when God humbled me. My wife was pregnant and had to stay in bed for three months because the baby's life was in jeopardy. I prayed for her but nothing seemed to happen. That's hard for a man with a healing ministry. My son was in the womb for five months and a few days after his birth he weighed only nineteen ounces. The doctors operated on him but didn't think he'd live.

## ■ To reflect

Think about any difficulties you have had in your life.

How did you respond at the time?

_____

With hindsight can you see what God was doing?

_____

## ■ To meditate on

The importance of humility.
'This is the one I esteem: he who is humble and contrite in spirit, and trembles at my word'
(Isa. 66:2b).
'God opposes the proud but gives grace to the humble' (1 Pet. 5:5b).

I was committed to make a month-long missionary journey to central Africa. Before I left, I visited my son in the intensive care unit. He was wired up to all kinds of monitors and was barely breathing. I anointed him with oil and left. I didn't know if I'd see him alive again. I felt mentally and spiritually stripped.

In Africa thousands of people came to our crusades. In Zaire they estimated that 118,000 were born again. During one meeting God gave me a word of knowledge about a man whose son had died at four o'clock that morning. The boy's unbelieving uncle watched over the body at the hospital some distance from the crusade ground. At the moment I prayed the boy sneezed twice and awoke as if from sleep!

When I got home I discovered that the Lord had restored my son as well. Now I look back at the amazing things that happened during those meetings and I know that the stripping process was worth it.

There's always a reason behind a season of stripping. You may not understand it all, but God is working things out and He's faithful. Trust Him. He will give you new revelation of Himself and bring glory to His name.

## ■ Food for thought

➢ Read Matthew 8:5–13.

➢ How does the centurion display humility?

➢ What is the end result?

➢ In what ways is the centurion a model for us when we come to Jesus for healing?

## ■ To question

What is humility?

Look up the dictionary definition and then look up some references to humility in the Bible.

Write down your own definition of what it is to be humble.

_____

_____

Does this describe you?

**A true understanding and humble estimate of oneself is the highest and most valuable of all lessons.**
_Thomas à Kempis_

# The dipping process

N aaman stood in the river. His leprous body must have been a horrible sight as he dipped himself in the water. After about the fourth time, I can imagine the devil saying to him, 'Give up. It's not going to work. Nothing's happening.' But Naaman had been given a word from God and he persisted. When he came up the seventh time, he was completely healed.

Today God says to us, 'Go on. Obey my Word. Dip seven times.' Seven is the perfect number. Some of us have dipped three times and stopped because we think, 'It's not going to work.' But the principle isn't: dip a little, get a little — much as we'd prefer it that way. God calls us to press through in faith until He gives us the healing, the finances or the help that we long to receive.

You may be standing there with Naaman — stripped and out on a limb. Maybe you're embarrassed and hurting and wondering if you've got the strength to go on. The devil is doing all he can to steal the blessing that will come to you if you continue trusting the Word of God. 'You're defeated,' he says. 'It's time to quit.' But God urges you to rise up in faith and to believe Him for breakthrough.

## ■ To understand

When we are experiencing difficulties we are often tempted to stop praying, studying and worshipping the Lord.

However, faith comes through hearing the Word of God. So it is important that we take every opportunity to listen.

If you are discouraged, talk to the Lord about it and ask Him to speak to you from His Word.

## ■ To meditate on

The Bible encourages us to persevere. 'Let us not become weary in doing good, for at the proper time we will reap a harvest if we do not give up' (Gal. 6:9).
'Let us throw off everything that hinders and the sin that so easily entangles, and let us run with perseverance the race marked out for us' (Heb. 12:1b).

While I was in Africa, my wife received a phone call from the man who was heading up the crusade. 'Thank you so much for allowing your husband to come to us,' he said. Then he explained some of the amazing things that had been happening.

As Bonnie listened, she began to weep. She had been struggling to keep going and now she was being told what God had done because of our faith. Suddenly the sacrifices she had made seemed insignificant. God had glorified His name and that was all that mattered.

God can transform any situation, but the way He does it is unlikely to be easy. Naaman was willing to remove the layers and humble himself. Like him, we must be willing to be stripped of anything that will prevent God from blessing us and bringing glory to His name.

The Lord can only use us powerfully as we co-operate with Him. He's looking for people who will allow Him to deal with their pride and selfishness. He's looking for people who press through and find deliverance through faith in His Word. He's looking for people who want not just healing but a mighty new revelation of Himself. Are you one of them?

➤ Using a concordance, find as many Scriptures as you can which encourage you about healing or witnessing or a subject of your choice.

➤ Write them down in a notebook and memorise one each day for the next week or two.

➤ As you are speaking the Word of God to yourself, your faith will increase and you will be encouraged to press on with God.

■ **To do**

Why not start a prayer diary?

Write down what you are praying for and the date in a notebook. Later go back and write in when your prayer has been answered.

You will be amazed as you look back through it and see how your prayers have been answered. It will encourage you to be consistent and to persevere in prayer.

**We must be followers of those who through faith and patience inherited the promises, and we must let God's furnace refine and prepare us for the ministry that he has for us in the future.**
*Terry Virgo*

# The blood of the Lamb

'I will pass through Egypt and strike down every firstborn ... and I will bring judgment on all the gods of Egypt ... The blood will be a sign for you on the houses where you are; and when I see the blood, I will pass over you. No destructive plague will touch you when I strike Egypt' (Exod. 12:12,13).

I once had a vision of thousands of oppressed people who had vampire bat creatures clinging to them. On the backs of these bats there were names: divorce, addiction, cancer, abortion, depression, suicide — and they were feeding off the people. Everyone was in pain and was trying to get free. Then suddenly a beautiful woman in white stood up. She raised her hands against the bats who caught fire and began screaming. Then they shrivelled up and the people were totally delivered.

I asked the Lord, 'Who is that woman and what's she doing?' And He replied, 'She's my bride and she's sprinkling my blood over the demons who think she's powerless.'

The Israelites were given a revelation of the blood of Jesus when they were in bondage in Egypt. The Egyptians were cruel taskmasters and for 450 years the Israelites had to endure terrible poverty and oppression. Then God told them that He would deliver them. He commanded them to put the blood of a lamb on the doorframes of their houses and to eat the meat. Then He promised that when the destroying angel passed over them, none of them would be harmed.

## ■ To consider

How does the Passover foreshadow what Jesus did?

_____

_____

_____

## ■ To meditate on

We are called to be overcomers. 'For everyone born of God overcomes the world. This is the victory that has overcome the world, even our faith' (1 John 5:4).
'To him who overcomes, I will give the right to sit with me on my throne, just as I overcame and sat down with my Father on his throne' (Rev. 3:21).

Four million Israelites came out of Egypt with great wealth and in perfect health. 'He brought them forth also with silver and gold: and there was not one feeble person among their tribes' (Ps. 105:37 AV). That's the power of the blood of the Lamb! It's mighty! When you understand that, you won't be afraid and you won't tolerate failure.

The enemy feeds on negative energy. He loves to see depression, discord and discouragement and seeks to multiply them. If we try to shake him off on our own, we will never succeed. But we were never destined to defeat the devil in our strength. We overcome him only 'by the blood of the Lamb and by the word of [our] testimony' (Rev. 12:11a).

We will see victory only when we stand up and appropriate the mighty blood of Christ. If members of your family are unsaved, raise your hands over their beds and by faith 'sprinkle' the blood. If your boss or work colleagues aren't Christians, lay your hands on their chairs and do the same. Don't let the devil convince you that it's useless. Every demon in hell trembles over the blood and every believer on earth should be overcoming through it.

➢ Write out in a notebook your testimony of how God has:

- healed you
- provided for you
- directed you
- spoken to you
- protected you, etc.

➢ When you are attacked by the devil remind yourself of what God has done for you.

## ■ To resolve

Resolve now that you will appropriate the blood of Jesus in your own life.

Write down in what ways you need to do this.

_____

_____

_____

_____

**Our salvation lies in looking away to the Lord Jesus and in seeing that the Blood of the Lamb has met the whole situation created by our sins and has answered it. That is the sure foundation on which we stand.**
_Watchman Nee_

# It is finished

(Jesus) had to be made like his brothers in every way, in order that he might become a merciful and faithful high priest in service to God, and that he might make atonement for the sins of the people (Heb. 2:17).

Since we have a great high priest who has gone through the heavens, Jesus the Son of God, let us hold firmly to the faith we profess. For we do not have a high priest who is unable to sympathise with our weaknesses, but we have one who has been tempted in every way, just as we are — yet was without sin (Heb. 4:14,15).

As I've already mentioned, the number seven stands for perfection in the Bible. I'd like to look more closely at this than I already have.

On one day in the year the high priest would go into the Holy of Holies to atone for the Israelites. He would take the blood of a sacrificial animal and sprinkle it seven times before the altar (Lev. 16:14,16) and God would forgive their sins. The blood protected and delivered them, but not permanently because the same sacrifice had to be repeated year after year. One day another High Priest would offer Himself as the perfect sacrifice for sin and His people would be redeemed for ever.

The high priest in Israel sprinkled the blood seven times and Jesus shed His blood for us in seven ways. We read: 'his sweat was like drops of blood' (Luke 22:44b); He 'offered [His] cheeks to those who pulled out [His] beard' (Isa. 50:6); 'they ... struck him with their fists. Others slapped him' (Matt. 26:67); 'Pilate ... had Jesus flogged' (Mark 15:15b); '[They]... twisted together a crown of thorns and set it on his head ... and took the staff and struck him on the head again and again' (Matt. 27:29a,30b); 'they crucified him' (Mark 15:24a); 'one of the soldiers pierced

## ■ To assess

What implications does the phrase 'it is finished' have for you in the way that you live your life?

## ■ To meditate on

What the blood of Jesus has done for us.
'For God was pleased ... through him to reconcile to himself all things ... by making peace through his blood, shed on the cross' (Col. 1:19a,20).
'And the blood of Jesus, his Son, purifies us from all sin' (1 John 1:7b).

Jesus' side with a spear, bringing a sudden flow of blood and water' (John 19:34).

But God points us beyond the perfect number to the perfect sacrifice. From the cross, Jesus said, 'It is finished' (John 19:30a) The Greek word He used speaks of doing something 'completely complete'. Jesus has fully satisfied the Father on our behalf. We can't manufacture our own righteousness because we are already righteous in Him (Rom. 4:23,24). Jesus triumphed at Calvary so that in Him we can win the victory over anything that enslaves, oppresses or frightens us.

So you no longer need to live in sin because Christ's death has freed you from its grip (Rom. 4:6,7). Call upon Him. Believe by faith that He has conquered and you will conquer with Him. Certainly, you will have to struggle against temptation, but because Jesus overcame it, so too can you. His power is yours.

You need have no fear of the devil either. He couldn't touch Jesus, so if you are in Him, he can't touch you either. You have been given complete authority over the evil one. So trample down his strongholds and seek to establish the Kingdom of God wherever you go.

➤ Read Hebrews 9— 10:18.

➤ In a notebook draw a line down the centre of a page. In the left-hand column write down the features of the Old Testament sacrificial system and in the right-hand column, the corresponding features of Jesus' work on the cross, e.g. the blood of bulls and goats/Jesus' own blood.

➤ Spend time thanking God for His wonderful provision for us.

## ■ To recognise

'We should no longer be slaves to sin'! (Rom. 6:6b)

Recognise that you are dead to sin but alive to Christ.

You are free from the power of sin so don't let it rule over you.

Don't put yourself in the place of temptation.

When you understand that, every time the devil comes at you with his shouts of defiance and his lies about your past, present and future, you hold the key to life or death by what you believe and by what you say, *then* you'll truly prize the word of your testimony.
*Larry Lea*

# Pay attention!

He who has the Son has life; he who does not have the Son of God does not have life (1 John 5:12).

You know the grace of our Lord Jesus Christ, that though he was rich, yet for your sakes he became poor, so that you through his poverty might become rich (2 Cor. 8:9).

W hat does the Bible mean by 'abundant life'? After all, plants have life and so do insects, birds, fish and mammals. Unbelievers have life too. But the life that God wants us to enjoy is different from pure existence and has little to do with externals. Rather it's a supernatural energy that wells up from within. It's rich, victorious and eternal. Sadly, we often fail to experience it to the full.

In the 1940s there was a poor farmer who owned a remote and totally unproductive reservation in Oklahoma. Then a huge deposit of oil was discovered under his land and overnight he became one of the wealthiest men in America. Now he'd noticed that rich people drove around in Cadillacs so he said, 'I'm going to buy the biggest Cadillac that anyone has ever seen.' The car was custom-made. It was so long that it had six wheels and he used to sit in it. But he couldn't turn the ignition and speed off down the highway because he'd never learnt to drive. Eventually he hitched two horses to the front of the car and let them pull him along.

Too many of us do the same thing. We receive the Word of life and overnight we become millionaires in Christ. Suddenly we

■ **To discover**

How does Jesus describe someone who hears His words and puts them into practice? (Luke 6:46–49)

Which of the two men in this story is most like you?

Is your attitude to the Word of God one of faith?

Ask the Lord for the gift of faith.

■ **To meditate on**

The value of the Word.
'All Scripture is God-breathed and is useful for teaching, rebuking, correcting and training in righteousness, so that the man of God may be thoroughly equipped for every good work' (2 Tim. 3:16,17).
'Do not merely listen to the word, and so deceive yourselves. Do what it says' (James 1:22).

realise that we have His mighty power to overcome our weaknesses and destroy the devil's strongholds, but we don't live in the good of it. There we are, plodding along with our two horses while the Spirit's crying, 'Turn on the ignition! There's a 100-horsepower engine under the bonnet. Use it!'

The source of power is the Word of God. By believing it we receive salvation. By continuing to trust it, we experience abundant life. Unfortunately many believers read their Bibles and listen to sermons with closed ears. They allow the devil to steal the truth from them and agree with him that 'much of what's written in the Bible really isn't for today.' In this way they rob themselves of God's blessings both to them and through them to others.

Jesus' words are 'life' (John 6:63b) and the Lord urges us, 'pay attention to what I say' (Prov. 4:20a). He promised the Israelites that He would keep them in good health on condition that they listened to Him and kept His decrees (Exod. 15:26). As we listen and obey the Word, faith will rise in our hearts and we will live in the good of everything that Jesus died to give us.

## ■ Food for thought

➢ Read through Psalm 119.

➢ Underline or make a note of each time the Psalmist refers to the Word (decrees, statutes, law, teaching, etc.).

➢ What importance does the Psalmist attach to the Word of God?

➢ What benefits does the Word bring to us? For example, a lamp to my feet — it gives direction.

## ■ To analyse

Do you need to 'turn on the ignition'?

Write down one specific way in which you can begin to do this.

_____

_____

_____

Ask the Lord to help you; don't let this opportunity pass or you will be hearing and not doing the Word.

If our passion for truth does not imply a passion for obedience to truth, then we are not really serious about it.
Bruce Milne

# Inherit the promises

His divine power has given us everything we need for life and godliness through our knowledge of him who called us by his own glory and goodness. Through these he has given us his very great and precious promises, so that through them you may participate in the divine nature and escape the corruption in the world caused by evil desires (2 Pet. 1:3,4).

The Bible tells us that we have all the resources we need to live an abundant and effective life. This provision is found in the promises of God.

God fulfilled His promises to Israel, but the people had to do something to secure them. It would have been pointless their staying in the wilderness and declaring, 'Hallelujah! God has given us the Promised Land.' Under Joshua, they had to go in and take possession of it. God didn't fill in all the blanks. He didn't remind His people that there were giants standing on the promises and give them explicit instructions about how to deal with them. He simply said, 'The land is yours. Take it!'

Today Jesus leads His New Covenant people into their inheritance — the land of promises. He knows that we will encounter the giants but isn't going to tell us how to overcome them until we've moved forward. His focus isn't on the problems but on the promises. 'Go in!' He urges us. 'I will give you every place where you set your foot' (Josh. 1:3).

We read, 'no matter how many promises God has made, they are "Yes" in Christ' (2 Cor. 1:20a). Jesus fulfils every one of them for us.

## ■ To question

What is a promise?

'Assurance given to a person that one will do or not do something' *Concise Oxford Dictionary.*

That assurance is only of value if the person making the promise is to be trusted.

The promises of God, therefore, are absolutely certain.

## ■ To meditate on

The Lord is faithful.
'God is not a man, that he should lie, nor a son of man, that he should change his mind. Does he speak and then not act? Does he promise and not fulfil?' (Num. 23:19)
'Let us hold unswervingly to the hope we profess, for he who promised is faithful' (Heb. 10:23).

That's a present-day reality, not just a future longing. And it's true not just for gifted people, but for all believers. The promises are dependent not on your personal circumstances — whether you're rich or poor — but solely on the Word of God. Once you've received Christ as your Saviour, all His promises become 'Yes' for you. Provision, peace, protection, power — they're all yours! But you must march into them. That's what abundant life is all about — living in the good of God's precious promises.

For a long time many of us have been pulled around by two horses in some area or another. We fail to believe God for financial provision, victory over temptation or help in difficult situations. 'I don't have the resources,' we think as we crack the whip and plod along the edge of God's promises.

I can imagine Jesus replying, 'Unhitch the horses, turn on the ignition and unleash my power. Move into the promises in my Word and fulfil the condition of obedience. Then I'll establish you in the land and give you victory over your "giants". Then my blessing will rest on everything that you have and do. And then you will experience life to the full.'

## ■ Food for thought

➤ One of the covenant names of God is the Healer.

➤ Using a concordance find as many promises as you can which relate to healing.

➤ What conditions, if any, are attached to these promises? What do these promises tell you about the Lord's willingness to heal?

➤ Next time you have an opportunity to pray for healing, remember these promises and believe that the Lord will fulfil them.

## ■ To appropriate

Are there giants in your life? Perhaps ...

- in your finances;
- you have an unsaved partner;
- you are experiencing opposition at work, etc.

Take one of the promises relevant to your situation — ask the Lord to fulfil His Word and see what He will do.

**The power to believe *a promise* depends entirely, but only, on faith in *the promiser*. Trust in the person begets trust in his word.**
*Andrew Murray*
*With Christ in the School of Prayer*

# His powerful Word

'Go into all the world and preach the good news to all creation. Whoever believes and is baptised will be saved, but whoever does not believe will be condemned. And these signs will accompany those who believe: In my name they will drive out demons; they will speak in new tongues; they will pick up snakes with their hands; and when they drink deadly poison, it will not hurt them at all; they will place their hands on sick people, and they will get well' (Mark 16:15–18).

We read that 'the word of God is living and active' (Heb. 4:12a), but many of us are totally oblivious of its power. That's because we have allowed the devil to bind us into fear, insecurity and low self-esteem. 'You're useless to God,' he tells us. And we believe him. So we hide behind locked doors, unmindful of the authority that we have to help a world of lost, desperate and hurting people.

Today, Jesus comes to us where we are and calls us to throw off the lies of the enemy and to fulfil our destiny. He's looking for an army who know the power of the Word, preach it and expect to see its impact on the lives of others.

One of my crusades was broadcast live on radio throughout Costa Rica, Panama and Nicaragua. Thousands were converted and healed at the crusade and at home. One lady testified on air, 'I was dying of a malignant tumour, the size of a grapefruit, which was growing in my throat. When I heard you preaching the Word on radio, the tumour started vibrating violently. Then suddenly it exploded and came out of my mouth. The next day I went to the clinic where they did eighteen X-rays but couldn't find any trace of it.'

## ▩ To consider

The Word of God is referred to as the Sword of the Spirit.

Think of ways in which you can use the Word as a sword.

## ▩ To meditate on

God's Word has impact.
'He sent forth his word and healed them' (Ps. 107:20a).
'So is my word that goes out from my mouth: It will not return to me empty but will accomplish what I desire and achieve the purpose for which I sent it' (Isa. 55:11).
'The word of God is ... sharper than any double-edged sword' (Heb. 4:12a).

Another woman had a malignant tumour on top of her head. She said that while she was listening to the broadcast, she felt a wetness go down her neck and thought that she was bleeding to death. Being too frightened to look, she wrapped a towel round her head and kept on listening. When she removed the towel, the tumour had totally gone.

A man who had suffered from a horrible skin condition for many years was also healed while he listened to the radio. He heard me say, 'God is healing someone who has a severe skin condition,' looked down at his hands and arms and watched new skin appear not only on them, but over his entire body.

The final day of the crusade was televised. Halfway through my message I looked up and saw tears streaming down the faces of the cameramen. When I gave an invitation for salvation, they abandoned their cameras and received Christ as their Saviour and Lord.

These things happen not because I'm special but because the Word is powerful. The Psalmist realised this. 'My heart trembles at your word', he said (Ps. 119:161b). Preach it and lives will be transformed.

> ➤ Imagine yourself to be one of the disciples crossing Lake Galilee (Mark 4:35–41).

> ➤ Picture a storm so severe that experienced fishermen fear for their lives! Feel their awe as Jesus speaks to the elements 'Quiet! Be still!'

> ➤ What other Scriptural examples are there of God speaking and power being released?

## ■ To respond

Paul asks 'How can they hear without someone preaching to them?' (Rom. 10:14b)

Talk to the Lord and ask Him to show you how you can begin to preach His powerful Word.

First, there is power in the Word of God. Power for salvation is not in man's wisdom but in God's Word. If men would be saved therefore, it is to God's Word that they must turn; and if preachers would exercise a saving ministry it is God's Word which they must preach.
*John Stott*

# The Holy Spirit and power

'You will receive power when the Holy Spirit comes on you; and you will be my witnesses in Jerusalem, and in all Judea and Samaria, and to the ends of the earth' (Acts 1:8).

'I will pour out my Spirit on all people. Your sons and daughters will prophesy, your old men will dream dreams, your young men will see visions. Even on my servants, both men and women, I will pour out my Spirit' (Joel 2:28,29).

After His baptism, Jesus was 'full of the Holy Spirit' (Luke 4:1a); after His temptation He 'returned to Galilee in the power of the Spirit' (Luke 4:14a). To do the works of Jesus we must be full of the Holy Spirit and power.

Jesus' entire ministry was characterised by power. It's no wonder that His disciples didn't want Him to leave them. They'd heard His amazing teaching and seen His mighty miracles. For three years their lives had been wrapped up in His and they could hardly bear the thought of being without Him. But Jesus couldn't remain with them. 'It is for your good that I am going away,' He told them. 'Unless I go away, the Counsellor will not come to you; but if I go, I will send him to you' (John 16:7).

When Jesus was on earth, He was limited by His physical body which couldn't be in two places at once. But one day He would pour out His Spirit on all people. Then He could be with every believer all the time. When He told His disciples to expect to receive His power, He was closing one era, and opening another. No longer would the anointing of God be upon selected individuals, but upon all His people regardless of their sex, colour or social standing.

## ■ To recall

Paul exhorts us to 'be filled with the Spirit'. A more accurate translation of this would be 'Be being filled with the Spirit'.

In other words we should make sure that we are continually filled with the Spirit and not simply as a one-off experience.

Make it your daily prayer that you will be filled with the Spirit.

## ■ To meditate on

The Baptism in the Holy Spirit.
'But after me will come one who is more powerful than I ... He will baptise you with the Holy Spirit and with fire' (Matt. 3:11b).
'If you ... know how to give good gifts to your children, how much more will your Father in heaven give the Holy Spirit to those who ask him!' (Luke 11:13)

Our first baby was a boy. Now let's imagine what might have happened just before we left the hospital.

Nurse: Here's your baby.

Me: But it's a girl!

Nurse: Does it matter? She's got two eyes, two hands, two legs. Why be fussy?

Me: But we want our son! Where is he?

On the day of Pentecost a baby church was born. It was full of the Holy Spirit and power. There were miracles, prophecies, tongues, interpretations and healings. As it grew it matured, but it never changed in character.

Today some people say, 'Let's have this sort of church. All this supernatural stuff is a bit too much for us. But it doesn't matter. We can still love one another and witness for Christ.' And Jesus replies, 'That's not my church. It belongs to someone else. My church is full of miracles and power. Where is it?'

The church will be authentic only when believers take seriously Jesus' command to be baptised in the Holy Spirit and begin to move into the supernatural. If you haven't had that experience, seek God for it; if you have, ask Him to help you to exercise more power.

## ■ Food for thought

➢ Look at Matthew 3:16; John 3:8; 7:37–39; Acts 2:2–4.

➢ The Holy Spirit is likened to wind, fire, water and a dove. What characteristics of the Holy Spirit do these things suggest?

➢ Seek to know the Holy Spirit in full measure — as wind, fire, water and dove.

## ■ To pray

Spend 5 or 10 minutes praying in tongues.

'He who speaks in a tongue edifies himself' (1 Cor. 14:4a).

When you pray in tongues, the Holy Spirit is speaking to God on your behalf. You will find that you are brought straight into the presence of God.

Why not make this a part of your daily devotions?

The Holy Spirit is therefore none other than that member of the eternal Godhead who brings to bear in the life of God's people the fruits of the victory won by Christ in his life, death and glorification. The ministry of the Spirit is in this sense a 'spilling over' from the throne of God of the blessing wrought by Christ for sinners.
*Bruce Milne*

# Walk by the Spirit

As Jesus was coming up out of the water, he saw heaven being torn open and the Spirit descending on him like a dove. And a voice came from heaven: 'You are my Son, whom I love; with you I am well pleased' (Mark 1:10,11).

You are all sons of God through faith in Christ Jesus, for all of you who were baptised into Christ have clothed yourselves with Christ ... Because you are sons, God sent the Spirit of his Son into our hearts, the Spirit who calls out, '*Abba*, Father' (Gal. 3:26,27;4:6).

John the Baptist pointed to Jesus as the Lamb of God. The lamb represents purity, humility and sacrifice. When Jesus came out of the water a dove settled on Him. The dove is symbolic of the Spirit who will always descend on someone who is pure, humble and holy. We must welcome the Spirit just as Jesus did.

The Spirit is the key to our functioning in power. Now there's a paradox here. The Spirit will always remain with us and yet He will take flight if we fail to respond appropriately to Him. The Bible says that we can grieve Him, quench Him, lie to Him, ignore Him, disobey Him, blaspheme Him, resist and reject Him. On many occasions I've seen the dove descend on people but fail to stay because they've reacted wrongly. Many of them have been afraid of His activity and have deliberately shunned His work in their lives.

Today God wants to raise up an end-time army who know not only how to bring the dove down but make Him so comfortable that He stays. Very few people have been able to do this consistently. The Moravians succeeded. For ninety-nine years they had a twenty-four hour prayer chain and their code was, 'One man at

## ■ To confess

Have you quenched the Holy Spirit? Perhaps you have dismissed the supernatural?

Confess it to the Lord.

Ask the Holy Spirit to reveal Himself to you and begin to cultivate a new relationship with Him.

## ■ To meditate on

Listen to the Spirit.
'Keep in step with the Spirit' (Gal. 5:25).
'Those who live in accordance with the Spirit have their minds set on what the Spirit desires' (Rom. 8:5b).
'Are you so foolish? After beginning with the Spirit, are you now trying to attain your goal by human effort?' (Gal. 3:3)
'Walk by the Spirit, and you will not carry out the desire of the flesh' (Gal. 5:16 NASB).

home; one man on the field.' It's probable that they were the most effective missionary movement in history.

I was raised in Kenya and I learnt two words in Swahili which both meant, 'Come'. The first was 'Kooja' and you employed it when you were speaking to people whom you didn't know that well. But the second word was 'Karibooni' and you used it to address your loved ones. So when you saw your friends and relatives and wanted them to stay, you would say, 'Karibooni' — 'From the depths of my heart I welcome you.'

We must be a company of people who know how to steward the visitations of God. There's a vast difference between saying, 'Holy Spirit, come upon us' and 'Holy Spirit, come and stay.' The Spirit is the key to salvation, healing and deliverance and God wants us to welcome Him. How do we do that? We seek the once-off experience of the baptism in the Spirit and then cultivate an intimate daily relationship with Him. We listen to His voice and do as He says. When the Spirit sees that we are pure, humble and holy, He will remain on us and manifest Jesus to us. And God will anoint us with power to do the same works that Jesus did.

> Find Scriptures which illustrate:

- grieving
- quenching
- lying to
- ignoring
- disobeying
- resisting
- rejecting

the Holy Spirit.

■ **To question**

How can you cultivate an intimate relationship with the Holy Spirit?

_____

_____

Is this your experience?

Then the Lord said something to me that totally changed my life, 'You must get to know and work with the Holy Spirit!'
I knew I was born again. I knew I was filled with the Holy Spirit. Yet, I had always thought of the Holy Spirit as an experience and not as a personality.
*Paul Y. Cho*

# When you fast

'When you fast, do not look sombre as the hypocrites do, for they disfigure their faces to show men they are fasting ... they have received their reward in full. But when you fast, put oil on your head and wash your face, so that it will not be obvious to men that you are fasting, but only to your Father, who is unseen; and your Father, who sees what is done in secret, will reward you'
(Matt. 6:16–18).

T he disciples had a problem. They'd prayed for a demonised boy but he wasn't delivered. When Jesus arrived He told them, 'this kind does not go out except by prayer and fasting' (Matt. 17:21). Like the disciples, we will confront certain evil powers that will not budge unless we fast as well as pray.

Power is released when people fast. Islamic nations have found this. For one month a year they fast from dawn to sunset, and they release spiritual energy. If unbelievers can affect the spiritual climate for false gods, how much more should Christians be involved in fasting for the intervention of their God?

Some Christians protest, 'Fasting isn't commanded in the New Testament.' True. But Jesus clearly expected His disciples to continue the practice. He didn't say, 'If you fast ...' but 'When you fast ...' (Matt. 6:16a), and He assumed that His followers would fast after He had returned to heaven (Matt. 9:14,15) — which they did (e.g. Acts 13:1–3).

God challenged me about fasting many years ago when I was working in a home for mentally handicapped children. At the home was a sixteen-year-old boy with a mental age of about

■ **To realise**

'When you fast ... '
'Who, me?'
'Yes, you.'

Fasting is for any disciple of Jesus.

It is not only for pastors or 'mature' people but for anyone who wants to draw near to God and to see His power released.

■ **To meditate on**

The benefits of humility.
'He guides the humble in what is right and teaches them his way' (Ps. 25:9).
'Humble yourselves before the Lord, and he will lift you up' (James 4:10).
'He ... gives grace to the humble' (Prov. 3:34).

two. Something in him was driving him to inflict pain on himself. He was given electric shock treatment but only grew worse. Then his arms were put in splints so he couldn't beat himself. But when the other kids saw that he was vulnerable, they pushed him over and he smashed his face on the concrete. As he bled and wept on my shoulder, I questioned God, 'What can I do?' and He told me, 'This kind does not go out except by prayer and fasting.'

After fourteen days of fasting, I said to Stevie, 'I want to tell you that Jesus loves you and that He came to set the captives free.' Then I added, 'In the name of Jesus, you foul spirit, come out of him now.' Stevie was flung about five feet into the air and was completely delivered. I untied his hands and he began gently touching his face. Then he started weeping. For the first time he was free not to beat himself.

Not everyone is called to go on long fasts, but we all need to fast. It's a way of humbling ourselves before God, of finding refreshment and cleansing from sin. God calls us to be a humble, dependent people through whom His power can flow. Let me encourage you: learn to fast. You'll be amazed at what God will do.

> ➤ What is the purpose of fasting illustrated in each of the following groups of verses?
>
> Ezra 8:21; Isa. 58:3.
>
> Ezra 8:23; 2 Chr. 20:1–3.
>
> 1 Kings 21:27–29; Jonah 3:5,10.
>
> Isa. 58:6; Matt. 17:21.
>
> Dan. 9:3,21,22.

■ **To imagine**

Close your eyes and picture a brick wall ... arrows seem to bounce off it but a battering ram demolishes it.

When your prayers seem to be ineffective or you have a seemingly insurmountable problem you can harness the power of the battering ram — fasting.

Fasting combined with prayer not only brings clarity of mind and spirit, releasing the voice of the Holy Spirit to give direction. It is also important for gaining spiritual and material victories.
*Paul Y. Cho*

# How you fast

After fasting for forty days and forty nights, (Jesus) was hungry (Matt. 4:2).

Then Esther sent this reply to Mordecai: 'Go, gather together all the Jews who are in Susa, and fast for me. Do not eat or drink for three days, night or day. I and my maids will fast as you do' (Esther 4:15,16a).

Fasting is about detachment from the world and attachment to God. There are three kinds of fast in the Bible. The normal fast involves your drinking only water. The partial fast means you abstain from certain foods — helpful for those with medical problems. The absolute fast — from food and water — is often appropriate in the face of extreme situations. It's unwise to abstain from water for more than three days except in exceptional, God-ordained circumstances (e.g. Exod. 34:28).

I would encourage individuals to fast when they need God's help in a particular situation. But I'd also recommend fasting on a regular basis — once a week or month. Christians need to learn how to fast together too. We had a twenty-one-day church fast and met each morning from 5.00 until 7.00. It was an amazing time. The Holy Spirit hovered over us. People I thought would never change were totally transformed and revival came to us because of the power that was released.

Jesus' first statement about fasting deals with motive (Matt. 6:16–18). We must not fast to impress others with our spirituality, but to give ourselves more fully to God. The fast must

## ■ To beware

The Pharisees used to make sure that people knew that they were fasting. Jesus called them hypocrites.

When you fast it is between you and the Lord — there is no reason why anyone else should know about it.

Never boast about your discipline of fasting. The Lord sees what you do in secret and He will reward you accordingly.

## ■ To meditate on

Seek the Lord.
'Ask and it will be given to you; seek and you will find; knock and the door will be opened to you. For everyone who asks receives; he who seeks finds; and to him who knocks, the door will be opened' (Matt. 7:7,8).
'He rewards those who earnestly seek him' (Heb. 11:6b).

not only be centred on Him, but appointed by Him too. If you seek Him, He will show you when He wants you to fast.

If you haven't fasted before, don't try to run before you can walk. Miss two meals on one day each week for a month and drink only fruit juice. Then begin fasting for whole days, and pray when you would normally be eating. Once you've achieved several twenty-four-hour fasts, seek God about a longer period of time.

When you feel called to a fast of three days or more, don't stuff yourself beforehand. Rather, eat lighter meals and avoid caffeine for two days. If your last meal consists of fresh fruit and vegetables, you should avoid constipation. The first three days are usually the hardest. By the sixth day, you will feel stronger and more alert. By the ninth or tenth day, the hunger pains will be only a minor irritation. Your sense of concentration will be sharpened and you will feel as if you could continue fasting indefinitely.

The major work of fasting happens in a spiritual realm. You will be engaged in spiritual warfare throughout. Use the Ephesians 6 armour and don't be tempted to relax until the fast has ended.

## ■ Food for thought

➢ Read Matthew 4. At what stage of Jesus' ministry was this? Why do you think Jesus chose to fast?

➢ What does this tell us about the importance of fasting?

➢ What implications does this have for you in your ministry?

➢ Write down in a notebook how you intend to respond to this.

## ■ To realise

Things you should know about a longer fast:
• Weight loss will be about one or two pounds a day.
• You may experience bad breath, headaches, coldness, tiredness, weakness and dizziness.
• Meet these difficulties sensibly. Keep warm, move slowly and rest frequently.
• Break particularly long fasts with fruit juice, not full meals. On the second day, eat fruit, milk and yogurt, then go onto salads without dressing and cooked vegetables.
• It's an excellent opportunity to check your eating habits and to become more disciplined in them.

**More than any other single Discipline, fasting reveals the things that control us. This is a wonderful benefit to the true disciple who longs to be transformed into the image of Jesus Christ. We cover up what is inside us with food and other good things, but in fasting these things surface.**
*Richard Foster*

## ❏ STUDY 16    **Follow me**

A man ... who was possessed by an evil spirit cried out, 'What do you want with us, Jesus of Nazareth? Have you come to destroy us? I know who you are — the Holy One of God!' 'Be quiet!' said Jesus sternly. 'Come out of him!' The evil spirit shook the man violently and came out of him with a shriek (Mark 1:23–26).

Jesus doesn't say to us, 'As the Father sent John Wesley, I am sending you.' He says 'As the Father has sent me, I am sending you' (John 20:21b). We praise God for pioneers like John Wesley, George Whitefield, Kathryn Kuhlman and Jim Elliott. They're great examples for us — as is the apostle Paul. Indeed, we are encouraged to imitate others (Heb. 6:12;13:7) and it's great that we've got Elijah/Elisha discipleship relationships in the church. But we must beware of focusing so much on our leaders that we forget that our ultimate model is Jesus Christ. He must always have the pre-eminence.

He's the model for our characters. If we're not careful, we can easily succumb to pride — particularly if God is blessing us. When Jesus was on earth, He knew that He was 'in very nature God' (Phil. 2:6a), but didn't appear among us as a mighty king. He came in the guise of a servant and taught, 'He who is least among you all — he is the greatest' (Luke 9:48b).

We must model our ministry on that of Jesus too. Wherever He went He preached the Word, healed and cast out demons. Before He arrived,

### ■ To resolve

How can we model ourselves on Jesus?

One simple way is to ask ourselves in every situation we face, 'What would Jesus do, say or think, etc.?'

If you resolve to do this and act upon it you will be following Jesus closely.

### ■ To meditate on

In His footsteps.
'Whoever serves me must follow me' (John 12:26a).
'Follow my example, as I follow the example of Christ' (1 Cor. 11:1).
'Christ suffered for you, leaving you an example, that you should follow in his steps' (1 Pet. 2:21b).

people were loaded down with evil spirits and there was really no way in which they could find deliverance. But when the Son of God appeared, the demons instinctively knew that their time was up. On several occasions they simply couldn't stand His presence and screamed out against Him.

If you are filled with the Holy Spirit and are trying to do the works of Jesus, evil spirits may sometimes cry out against you. When this happens, don't be surprised or fearful. Confront the enemy and learn from the experience. Jesus said, 'All authority in heaven and on earth has been given to me. Therefore go ... And surely I am with you always, to the very end of the age' (Matt. 28:18b,19a,20b). You have the promise of His power and His presence. Like Him, you can set people free.

Just as the Father sent Jesus, so Jesus is sending you. Model your life on His. Use whatever gifts He gives you to the glory of His name. I believe with all my heart that in these days God wants to release an army of men and women who will have the vision, the courage and the faith to do the same mighty works that His Son did.

➤ In a notebook write down ten character traits of Jesus that set an example for us. Use Scripture to back up each one, e.g. His humility — though He was God He humbled Himself 'taking the very nature of a servant' (Phil. 2:7). We should humble ourselves and serve one another.

➤ Pray through each of these areas asking the Lord to help you follow Jesus' example more fully.

## ■ To beware

It is easy for us to fall into the trap of simply *being* like Jesus — modelling our characters on Him and yet not *doing* the things He did.

We put limits on the way we follow Him because we dismiss ourselves. But Jesus has given us the power and the authority to do the works He did and even greater works.

Are *you* seeking to follow Jesus' example in every way?

**When Jesus called His disciples to follow Him, He wanted them to follow His example, both in life and ministry. They were to proclaim the Kingdom in word and power. And He was uncompromising in teaching what He expected of disciples.**
*Colin Urquhart*

# Good news to the poor

'The Spirit of the Lord is on me, because he has anointed me to preach good news to the poor' (Luke 4:18a).

'Is not this the kind of fasting I have chosen: to loose the chains of injustice and untie the cords of the yoke, to set the oppressed free and break every yoke? Is it not to share your food with the hungry and to provide the poor wanderer with shelter — when you see the naked, to clothe him, and not to turn away from your own flesh and blood?' (Isa. 58:6,7)

When the Holy Spirit visits us, He gives us a heart for the poor. He stirs a deep concern for those who are broken and hurting, who are in the grip of drugs, drink, violence or homosexuality. This passion will compel us to reach out to the defenceless and bring justice to the oppressed.

Once I was due to conduct an evening crusade in Pakistan. That morning I saw a woman in her sixties who had no eyeballs. She was sitting near a sewage outlet where there was raw sewage running very close to her. When I saw her, my heart broke. I thought, 'God, this is one of the poorest cities in one of the poorest countries in the world. Who will look after a poor blind woman?' I was so moved that I took a photo of her.

That evening I preached and then prayed, 'Father, reveal to these people that Jesus is Your Son. Show them that You have raised Him from the dead.' I began praying for people who were lining up at the front. Now sometimes, I sense such an anointing from God that I enter the ozone layer! That happened on this occasion. I was absorbed in prayer when suddenly my concentration was broken by a

## ■ To pray

The key to any ministry is the anointing of the Holy Spirit.

Spend time asking the Lord to anoint you for ministry.

Start taking the opportunity to pray for people you meet.

## ■ To meditate on

We should care for the poor.
'If a man shuts his ears to the cry of the poor, he too will cry out and not be answered' (Prov. 21:13).
'The righteous care about justice for the poor, but the wicked have no such concern' (Prov. 29:7).

noise. Initially I was irritated that someone had disturbed me. Then I saw the poor blind woman walking onto the platform. She stood there and said, 'I was born blind but when this man started praying, I saw flashes of light. God has given me eyes where there were none.' Later, I took another photo of her. You put this and the earlier one side by side and there's no way you can doubt the mighty miracle of God.

After I'd preached at another crusade in Pittsburgh, several drug addicts, alcoholics and prostitutes came up for prayer. They were afraid. I said to one girl, 'Honey, you don't need to be afraid of Jesus.' And as I watched the Lord just took her in His arms. Then the demons surfaced and came out screaming. By the end, all of these hurting people were delivered, saved and baptised in the Holy Spirit. After the meeting one of the pastors said to me, 'I'm afraid of those sort of people.' I replied, 'Brother, you repent! God has commissioned you to bind up the brokenhearted.'

Jesus reached out to the poor. Do we have any excuse not to do the same? Pray that God will give you His heart of compassion for those that the world so easily forgets.

## ■ Food for thought

➢ Read Matthew 25:35–46. Identify those in your locality or amongst your circle of acquaintances:

- who are hungry
- who are strangers
- who need clothes
- who are sick
- who are in prison.

➢ Jesus says 'whatever you did for one of the least of these brothers of mine, you did for me' (v. 40). How do you respond to that?

## ■ To do

Find out if your church has a social programme. If not, get in touch with the Salvation Army or other local charities and go out with them once or twice as they visit the poor.

Listen to your feelings — probably prejudices and judgmental attitudes will surface.

Repent of any wrong attitudes and ask the Lord to sensitise you to the needs of these people.

**Jesus enjoyed a very special relationship with people, especially those on the fringe of society. He treated them with respect and extended to them unconditional, non-condemnatory acceptance.**
*Dave Andrews*

# Filled with compassion

As a father has compassion on his children, so the LORD has compassion on those who fear him; for he knows how we are formed, he remembers that we are dust (Ps. 103:13,14).

A man with leprosy came to (Jesus) and begged him on his knees, 'If you are willing, you can make me clean.' Filled with compassion, Jesus reached out his hand and touched the man (Mark 1:40,41).

C hristians often speak about the need for faith. Certainly it's very important, but faith works alongside compassion — and we tend not to hear so much about that.

Many years ago, God broke off a little piece of His compassionate heart and put it in me. From that moment, I didn't care what the traditionalists said or what obstructions lay in my way. I simply wanted to see people touched by God, saved and healed.

I came out of one healing meeting that I'd been conducting in a very poor country, and there on the edge of the crowd was a woman. She was crying as she came up to me. 'Man of God,' she said, 'I don't care about myself, but please would you pray for my little girl?'

Hiding behind her was her three-year-old daughter who was wearing only a dirty old T-shirt. The mother lifted this up and I saw that all over her small body were the most horrible boils that cut deep into her flesh. As the woman bent down, her shawl slipped and I could see that her arms, shoulders and chest were covered with some kind of terrible fungus-like leprosy. But she was concerned only for her little girl.

## ■ To do

What is compassion?

Write in a notebook a modern-day parable to illustrate compassion.

## ■ To meditate on

God is compassionate.
'He had compassion on them, because they were harassed and helpless' (Matt. 9:36).
'Praise be to ...the Father of compassion and the God of all comfort' (2 Cor. 1.3).
'The Lord is full of compassion and mercy' (James 5:11b).

I held them both in my arms and wept and prayed for them. As I walked away, she was crying and saying, 'Thank you, sir, thank you so much for leaving your family and coming to pray for us poor people.' Tears filled my eyes and the Lord said to me, 'You feel compassion for them? That's the compassion I feel for the world. My church has been hiding away from them like Elijah in the cave. But My heart is breaking for these poor people.'

God longs to touch those who are hurting. Many of them once came to what they thought was the church, but failed to find healing for their wounds. They didn't hear anyone proclaim the living Word. They didn't encounter Jesus, the one who is full of mercy and compassion. And they left.

When God touches you as He did me, your heart will break for the hurting and it won't matter whether they drive Mercedes cars and have posh homes, or eat out of the dustbin and smell terrible. You will reach out to all of them with the love of Jesus. Are you hiding in the cave? Come out! You have been called to the poor and oppressed. Feel God's heart of compassion and bring them into the Kingdom.

■ **To think**

Our feelings of compassion are often tainted by our own values. For example we find it easy to be compassionate to someone who is less well off than ourselves but what about someone who is very rich?

Think about your attitudes towards the rich and poor, sick and well, clean and dirty.

Ask the Lord to give you His compassion towards *anyone* who needs it.

I would always carry in my heart the ache that I felt as I watched my son suffer, the ache that God the Father felt as he watched Jesus suffer, and the compassion with which he looks upon all his children who are afflicted. Because of the pain I had carried in my heart for Ben, I would always have room in my heart for the pain of others.
*Mahesh Chavda*

# ❏ STUDY 19 — Freedom for the prisoners

When Jesus had called the Twelve together, he gave them power and authority to drive out all demons and to cure diseases, and he sent them out to preach the kingdom of God and to heal the sick (Luke 9:1,2).

Psychologists say that demons are just a figment of our imagination; Jesus doesn't agree. Throughout His earthly ministry, He acted as though they were very real. Let's look at some of His encounters with evil spirits.

On one occasion, Jesus was teaching in the synagogue at Capernaum. Everything was going smoothly when suddenly a man cried out in the middle of the meeting. Now he wasn't an insane criminal. He was just an ordinary person sitting there listening to the sermon, but he had an evil spirit that was tormenting him. Maybe it was the spirit of pornography, adultery, suicide or alcohol. We don't know. What we do know is that Jesus confronted it, rebuked it and cast it out (Mark 1:25–26).

In another synagogue Jesus encountered a woman who had been crippled for eighteen years. We'd probably have looked at her and concluded, 'Poor thing. Her back desperately needs healing.' But Jesus perceived that the root cause of her sickness was a spirit. No doctor would ever have been able to help her because she was bound by something supernatural. When Jesus set her free from it, she straightened up. It must have been the

## ▣ To reflect

Modern Western thinking denies the existence of the supernatural and/or spiritual realms. We live in a materialistic culture which asserts that nothing exists except matter.

Take time to reflect on whether you have taken on board this world view which is contrary to the Word of God.

## ▣ To meditate on

Jesus has power over everything. 'Jesus knew that the Father had put all things under his power' (John 13:3a). 'All authority in heaven and on earth has been given to me' (Matt. 28:18). 'At the name of Jesus every knee should bow' (Phil. 2:10a).

most wonderful moment of her life (Luke 13:10–17).

Not all illness is demon-related, but often the underlying cause of sickness, oppression and addiction is demonic. Evil spirits delight in causing as much suffering as they can. They will afflict millions of ordinary people, driving some of them to do the most terrible things — abuse their children, rape elderly people and even commit suicide. Many individuals open themselves up to demons by getting into drugs, pornography, abortion, alcoholism and New Age practices. Some of them know they need help and seek advice from accredited doctors and psychiatrists, but they can't get free because only Jesus can release them. And how will He do this? Through His people — through you.

Gone are the days when we cowered at the very mention of demons and whispered to one another, 'If we don't bother them, they won't bother us.' We can't turn our backs on those who are trapped in the snares of Satan, who are crying out for help that they can't find. They desperately need someone to say to them, 'In the name of Jesus, be loosed from your infirmity.' You have that authority — use it.

## ■ Food for thought

➤ Read the following accounts:

Matt. 8:28–34;9:32–34; Mark 1:21–28;9:14–27; Luke 11:14.

➤ What symptoms did these people have?

➤ How did Jesus minister to them?

➤ How did the demons respond to Jesus?

## ■ To read

Jesus won the battle by inflicting a mortal wound on Satan. The whole chilly area of the occult and the demonic was robbed of its power by Calvary. Christ is the conqueror over all the power of the Enemy, and on the cross he inflicted such a crushing defeat on the devil that whenever his name is named in faith, Satan is bound to flee. I have seen this time and time again in lives afflicted by demonic possession. The demons have to leave when commanded to do so in the name of the Victor.
*Michael Green*

Jesus came as a divine invader to destroy demons and release men and women to eternal life, which explains why the Lord's presence caused demons to tremble and fear. Jesus' ministry was marked by continual conflict with Satan and demons, for the purpose of establishing God's reign on earth.
*John Wimber*

# From darkness to light

For he has rescued us from the dominion of darkness and brought us into the kingdom of the Son he loves (Col. 1:13).

Demons aren't past history; they're present fact. And no one can deliver people from them except Jesus. I've seen the power of the Spirit come upon insane individuals in chains and instantly restore them to their right minds. I've seen drug addicts completely healed, their arms bearing no sign of the needle marks. Releasing captives is a glorious ministry. There's nothing like helping someone in torment to find complete freedom in Christ.

A university student came up to me after a meeting. She was under clear conviction of sin, but before she prayed for salvation she told me that a few days previously she'd had an abortion. 'I feel so depressed,' she said. Then she repented and received the Lord. Suddenly, she screamed, fell down and started writhing as if she were giving birth. The abortion had opened the door to a spirit of torment. But Jesus completely delivered her and baptised her in His Holy Spirit.

A couple brought their daughter to me. She was in her forties and for twenty years she'd been trying to commit suicide. Her parents had taken her from one institution to another and were now at their wits' end. 'Do you have any

## ■ To encourage

'The one who is in you is greater than the one who is in the world' (1 John 4:4b).

Don't just read this verse quickly and pass on. Think about what it really means for you.

How does this help you when you encounter evil powers?

## ■ To meditate on

We need to enlist in God's army. 'Put on the full armour of God so that you can take your stand against the devil's schemes. For our struggle is not against flesh and blood, but against the rulers, against the authorities, against the powers of this dark world and against the spiritual forces of evil in the heavenly realms' (Eph. 6:11,12).

word from the Lord?' they pleaded. 'Yes,' I replied. I went up to the woman and said, 'You demon of suicide come out of her in the name of Jesus.' The evil spirit left immediately. What the psychiatrists had failed to do in twenty years, the Holy Spirit did in two minutes.

There are only two Kingdoms in the universe: the Kingdom of darkness and the Kingdom of light. Immediately you become a Christian, you transfer your allegiance from Satan to Christ and all evil powers will hate you. From that moment you're in a battle against them and you must realise it.

Fear is not the appropriate response to the enemy. Christian soldiers don't construct a big fort and declare, 'We're going to stay here. We're afraid to go out.' Our army is on the move. It puts on God's armour and fights. It marches from nation to nation and remains unsatisfied until people in the four corners of the world have bowed the knee to Jesus.

God longs to see the gates of hell demolished and His people plundering enemy strongholds. He calls us from passive into aggressive mode, from fear to faith. Release the captives and marvel at the power of Jesus' name!

➤ Read Acts 5:16;16:16–18;19:11. Did the apostles have any difficulty in casting out demons? Was their power in any way inferior to that of Jesus?

➤ What power do we have?

## ■ To challenge

Will you change gear from passive to aggressive mode?

God wants you to be eager to do His work whether it is in prayer, evangelism, healing, deliverance, etc.

Express your willingness to do whatever God wants you to. Tell Him that you are ready to follow Him in your ministry and ask Him for His power to equip you.

Take any opportunity to pray for the oppressed.

Demons are serious business. You cannot play games with them; you must tell them to leave ... We are not off base if we go about doing good and healing all that are oppressed of the devil, anointed with power and the Holy Ghost we're following Jesus.
*Ernest Gruen*

# A defeated foe

T he leader of the enemy forces is Satan. He's called the accuser of the brothers, a liar, a murderer, a deceiver, a thief and a destroyer. His army comprises myriads of evil beings who, although they have no bodies, do have emotions — one of which is fear. These evil spirits feed on darkness, pain and depression. It's their job to torment people, so they prey on their victims, make them suffer physically and emotionally, and if possible, drive them to suicide.

As we have already seen, we defeat Satan's forces not by looking fearsome and snarling menacingly when we're on the battle lines. Human beings might be frightened by that sort of behaviour, but demons will only laugh. No, what makes them tremble is the blood of the Lamb and the word of our testimony (Rev. 12:11a). This verse goes on to say that God's people didn't 'love their lives so much as to shrink from death' (11b). In other words, there's a cost involved. Jesus paid the ultimate price, but we're called to follow Him and must not be afraid to give our lives for His sake.

We're living in the age of overcoming. One day, Jesus will return and utterly destroy the

## ■ To renounce

Renounce anything which has ensnared you — an addiction, habit, anger, lust, etc.

Ask the Lord to break its power over you.

You may want to ask someone else (your pastor, housegroup leader, etc.) to pray for you.

## ■ To meditate on

Nothing is too hard for our God.
'What is impossible with men is possible with God' (Luke 18:27).
'Great is our Lord and mighty in power' (Ps. 147:5a).
'Ah, Sovereign LORD, you have made the heavens and the earth ... Nothing is too hard for you' (Jer. 32:17).

evil one. But for the moment, it's the major task of the church to take ground from him.

When the charismatic movement first began, many of us experienced the power of the Holy Spirit to heal and deliver. But we failed to get to the root of many serious complaints like cancer, paralysis and addiction. In these days, however, I believe that God is telling us that this generation will see signs and wonders that have rarely been witnessed before. He wants to give us an anointing which will enable us to tread on the power of the evil one and manifest the mighty works of Jesus to the nations.

As I travel around the world, I stand amazed at God's miraculous power. Once, I was a thousand miles up the Congo river in the land of the pygmies. I went in the dry season, but on the second day there was a terrible rainstorm — a supernatural attack of the enemy. Well, I kept preaching and we were all soaked. At the close of the meeting hundreds came forward to receive Jesus as their Saviour and as they prayed, the rain stopped. Then suddenly, twelve cripples, eight of whom had been born that way, got up one by one and started walking. Is anything too hard for the Lord?

## ■ Food for thought

➤ Meditate on God's power. You can do this by first listing in a notebook what is impossible for man, e.g. controlling the weather, and then considering all that God can do. Use the verses in the last section to help you.

➤ Next you can think about anything that is powerful — the wind, electricity, etc. and then remember that the Lord is more powerful than any of these.

➤ Spend time meditating; don't rush through it. Meditation should involve chewing over something in your mind until you have looked at it from every angle.

## ■ To declare

Write out in a notebook several verses which speak about God's power, e.g. 1 Chr. 29:11,12; Jer. 10:12; Rom. 4:17b; 19–21.

Make a point of declaring these verses to yourself at different times during the day.

As you hear the Word of God it will inspire your faith and confidence in the Lord.

Don't say 'I can't' but rather 'God can!'

**Jesus shows us that we have no need to be afraid of Satan. Jesus went into the battle with confidence of victory so long as he remained trusting, obedient and dependent on the Spirit. We can go in the same fearlessness. We need only fear the devil when we cease fully to oppose him.**
*Michael Green*

# A Saviour with answers

'Go back and report to John what you hear and see: The blind receive sight, the lame walk, those who have leprosy are cured, the deaf hear, the dead are raised, and the good news is preached to the poor' (Matt. 11:4,5).

A t one time, John the Baptist was filled with doubts about Jesus and sent Him this message from prison: 'Are you the one who was to come, or should we expect someone else?' (Matt. 11:3).

People today ask similar questions. They're imprisoned by their sin but are hungry for reality. 'Does Jesus really have the answer or should I look to something else?' they say. 'New Age sounds promising. Maybe I should try that. Perhaps I need to experiment a bit with drugs. What about pursuing more exciting sexual experiences? Or is life just about making as much money as I can?'

When Naaman went to the king of Israel to be cured of his leprosy, the king couldn't help him. The world has no answer to the needs of humanity. Naaman would have gone home disappointed if Elijah had not sent a message to the king which said, 'Make the man come to me' (2 Kings 5:8b). He alone could help Naaman and Jesus alone gives hope to mankind. 'Come to me,' He says to the weary and burdened, 'and I will give you rest' (Matt. 11:28).

We're Jesus' representatives, but sadly unbelievers have often failed to find the answer

## ■ To challenge

Do you believe with all your heart that Jesus has the answer, for you, your family, your friends, the nation, etc.?

If so it should motivate you to share the gospel with everyone around you.

If this is not true of you, what is stopping you?

## ■ To meditate on

Come to Jesus.
'Listen, listen to me ... Give ear and come to me; hear me, that your soul may live' (Isa. 55:2b,3a).
'Jesus answered "I am the way and the truth and the life"' (John 14:6a).
'If anyone is thirsty, let him come to me and drink' (John 7:37b).

with us. Many of our churches bear His name but don't demonstrate much of His character and power. They read about His compassion but have no real heart for the poor, the weak, the hungry, the sick and the dying. They've become content. They enjoy their worship times and dabble in witnessing, but they don't reflect the dynamic life of Jesus.

Of course, this is not the case with all our churches. Many of us are zealous for the Lord, and I praise God for the wonderful teaching that we hear about Him. But I also know that God longs for His people to experience more than head knowledge alone. He wants to give us a fresh revelation of the person of the Lord Jesus as someone who really does meet the needs of the world.

When Jesus replied to John the Baptist, He drew attention not so much to His teaching as to His miracles. In other words, His prime focus was on His ability to help everyone who came to Him. The role of the church is to point people not to a great teacher who appears in an ancient book, but to a glorious Saviour who has the answers to their problems and who is active on their behalf.

➤ Read 1 Kings 18: 16–40. Where does Elijah's confidence lie?

➤ What does that teach us?

➤ The prophets of Baal were disappointed because their god did not answer them. How can we demonstrate to people today that our God will answer and theirs will not?

■ **To consider**

What are the big problems which people face today?

_____

_____

Think about how Jesus is the answer to each of these and be ready to explain what He can do when you next meet anyone in these situations.

**Jesus is the answer for the world today,
Above him there's no other
Jesus is the way.**
*Andrae Crouch*
*'Jesus is the Answer'*

# This same Jesus

J esus hasn't changed. His Word hasn't changed. His will hasn't changed. So if He performed mighty signs two thousand years ago, He can do them now.

I've seen the miracle power of God transform thousands of people across the nations — and their cure is permanent. A while ago I met a man who was healed at one of my meetings. He was blind then and arrived with his guide dog. I prayed for him, he fell under the power of the Holy Spirit and when he got up he looked at me and said, 'I can see. Your coat's blue and my dog's black.'

Sometimes the people whose illness returns have made the mistake of divorcing the healing from the Healer. I've prayed for individuals who have been instantly delivered from cancers. The tumours have totally disappeared and so has the pain. They've been to doctors who have confirmed that they're healed but after a while, the disease comes back.

Once people receive healing they must hold onto the Healer. That means that when they've discovered a living relationship with the Lord Jesus, they mustn't go back to living the same way as they did before. By turning away from

## ■ To motivate

If all that Jesus said is true *and* He never changes, what are you waiting for?

You have the promise of His Word, the power of the Holy Spirit and faith which is the gift of God.

Jesus said that *you* can do even greater works than He did.

## ■ To meditate on

God is eternal.
'Your throne, O God, will last for ever and ever' (Ps. 45:6).
'"I am the Alpha and the Omega," says the Lord God, "who is, and who was, and who is to come, the Almighty"' (Rev. 1:8).

Jesus, they may find that the need for healing will arise again. So if God touches you, lay hold of His grace and don't let go.

I'm not the Healer. I know that I have no power of my own to deliver people from their sicknesses. I just exercise the gifts of healing and miracles.

Some years ago I was ministering in the open air in Zambia. Sitting in a wheelchair at the crusade was a boy of sixteen who had contracted polio when he was six months old. I prayed for him and also for a man whose legs had been curled under him all his life. Then I walked up the hill to pray for others.

Suddenly, there was a mighty roar and lots of applause from the crowd. The crippled man was shouting and jumping up and down on ankles that were now straight, and the teenager was running around. This boy's mother fell to the ground in front of me, put dust on her head and said, 'Thank you, great chief, for coming and healing my son.' I took her hand, raised her up and replied, 'I want you to know that I'm just a little servant of the greatest of chiefs and His name is Jesus. You must thank and worship Him.'

■ **Food for thought**

➢ Make a list in a notebook of the different types of miracles performed by Jesus.

➢ How many of these have you heard about or seen happen recently? Why do you think it is that most churches are not seeing miracles today?

■ **To realise**

When you pray for sick people why is it important to remember who is healing them?

_____

_____

... **we need to know that there are no limits to what God may choose to do to — and through — us. I challenge you to study these miracles of Jesus not as ancient history, but as a prelude to what He wants to do through you.**
Jamie Buckingham

# We have authority

He called his twelve disciples to him and gave them authority to drive out evil spirits and to heal every disease and sickness (Matt. 10:1).

'All authority in heaven and on earth has been given to me. Therefore go and make disciples of all nations ... And surely I am with you always, to the very end of the age' (Matt. 28:18b,19a,20b).

Do you see how Jesus multiplied His ministry? He began alone and then became the model for twelve disciples. They listened to Him and watched Him work. Then one day He gave them authority to heal and cast out demons and sent them to the Jewish people.

Jesus always equips His servants with power before He sends them out. Sadly, we often try to rely on human wisdom and intellect to see us through. Christians think that their Bible knowledge will qualify them for ministry. They go off to the mission field with high expectations, encounter supernatural forces and are scared stiff. They see people in the grip of demons and don't know what to do. Eventually they return home totally devastated.

The twelve disciples went with Jesus' anointing, so did the seventy-two. Jesus involved more and more of His disciples in powerful effective ministry. When this second group returned, they were full of joy that even the demons submitted to them in Jesus' name (Luke 10:1–17).

That's how you feel when you're moving in power — joyful. You'll be excited when alcoholics who have been tormented for thirty years are delivered in one minute. You'll be

## ■ To comprehend

Look up the word 'authority' in a dictionary and write down its definition.

_____

_____

_____

Jesus has given you the authority to overcome demons, sickness, addictions, etc.

## ■ To meditate on

God's plan is to use His church. 'His intent was that now, through the church, the manifold wisdom of God should be made known to the rulers and authorities ... according to his eternal purpose which he accomplished in Christ Jesus' (Eph. 3:10,11).

amazed when the lame walk, the deaf hear and the blind see. You'll be overjoyed when you see individuals who have been hostile to God bow the knee to Him. It's so rewarding to do the works of Jesus. You'll love it!

Jesus' authority now extends to all His disciples and His vision embraces not just the Jews, but the whole world. Our job description is the same as it was for the twelve and the seventy-two. We are commissioned to preach the good news and perform the signs that will prove that the Kingdom of God has come.

It doesn't matter whether you're a man or a woman, Jesus wants you involved. Some teaching tries to devalue women. It suggests that their primary job is to stay at home and do things like flower arranging. Now I believe in godly authority in the home with the husband as the head of the wife, but God hasn't deactivated fifty per cent of His army. His anointing rests on everyone. If we don't take our place, there'll be gaps in our ranks which will weaken us when we confront the enemy.

When Jesus ascended, He left the destiny of the world in the hands of His disciples. He's relying on us to complete what He has begun.

## ■ Food for thought

➤ 'Don't just sit there — do something!'

➤ How can you take up the authority God has given you?

➤ Write down in a notebook three specific ways in which you can begin to exercise it in your daily life.

## ■ To consider

Re-read Matthew 28:18–20. Notice that Jesus commissions us on the basis of His authority.

Ask God for fresh revelation of these verses.

Jesus made so much spiritual power available to the disciples; and yet faith and obedience had to be exercised or they would not be able to avail themselves of the authority at their disposal. Put very simply, because they were children of the Kingdom Jesus was teaching them a simple truth; whatever I can do you also can do.
*Colin Urquhart*

# Come, Holy Spirit!

I pray also that the eyes of your heart may be enlightened in order that you may know ... his incomparably great power for us who believe. That power is like the working of his mighty strength, which he exerted in Christ when he raised him from the dead and seated him at his right hand in the heavenly realms (Eph. 1:18a,19,20).

So shall they fear the name of the LORD from the west, and his glory from the rising of the sun. When the enemy shall come in like a flood, the Spirit of the LORD shall lift up a standard against him. (Isa. 59:19 AV).

**M**any Christian leaders are desperate to see the power of God moving in their congregations. When I was conducting a crusade in Costa Rica, I was asked to minister to the largest church in San Jose. I was reluctant because it was a very staid and proper church and I didn't want to create problems for the pastor.

When I spoke to him I warned him of the things that might happen. 'If I come, I'm not going to hold back,' I told him. 'I won't compromise what the Holy Spirit is telling me to do.' He listened but wouldn't be put off. 'My people are dead,' he replied. 'We need help. Please come.'

So I preached for him and then I invited the Holy Spirit to move among the people. Individuals everywhere began falling down under the power of God and getting up healed. The pastor was watching and weeping. He was so hungry to see the works of Jesus.

Then he came up to me accompanied by a very sophisticated lady and her nine-year-old son. She'd just been talking to him in Spanish, telling him, 'I don't believe in Jesus. But I just happen to be here today and I'm wondering if

## ■ To ask

What do we or our churches do which hinders the work of the Holy Spirit?

_____

_____

How can we make room for Him to work?

_____

## ■ To meditate on

The gifts of the Spirit.
'To one there is given through the Spirit the message of wisdom, to another the message of knowledge ... to another faith ... to another gifts of healing ... to another miraculous powers, to another prophecy, to another distinguishing between spirits, to another speaking in different kinds of tongues, and to still another the interpretation of tongues' (1 Cor. 12:8–10).

this man could pray for my son. He's totally dominated by fear.' The pastor explained to me that the son was petrified all the time and refused to go out of the house.

I stretched out my hand but placed it on the head of the mother, not the son. Then, acting on the Spirit's discernment, I said, 'You demon of witchcraft, come out of her now in the name of Jesus.' Suddenly she started hissing like a snake and tearing at her flesh and hair. People around her scattered in fear, but I began to laugh. Then I said, 'Satan, your time is up. Let her go.' The woman fell under the power of the Spirit and I told the pastor, 'Right, now you finish the work while I pray for other people.'

A few moments later I returned. The woman was lying on the floor with her hands raised in the air and tears mixed with mascara rolling down her face. She'd received Jesus and the baptism of the Holy Spirit right there on the floor and was worshipping the Lord in tongues. It was a glorious sight.

The power of Jesus isn't restricted to crusades. The Holy Spirit will work wherever He's invited. As churches and as individuals we've just got to begin making room for Him.

## ■ To equip

'Eagerly desire spiritual gifts' (1 Cor. 14:1b).

Ask the Holy Spirit to equip you with spiritual gifts to help you minister in the power of the Spirit.

## ■ Food for thought

➢ Over the next few weeks read an account of a revival, e.g. The Welsh Revival.

➢ Take particular note of the effect of the Holy Spirit in people's lives.

➢ Pray for the Holy Spirit's work in your own church.

**The Spirit is not a 'ghost', an eerie or arbitrary agency. He is the 'Spirit of Jesus' (Acts 16:7) who comes to minister Christ to the Christian community. Alarm at an *authentic* ministry of the Spirit needs the reassurance the disciples received when they saw Jesus walking on the sea of Galilee and cried out for fear it was a ghost: 'Take courage! It is I. Don't be afraid.'**
*Bruce Milne*

# Greater things than these

From the moment I turned from Hinduism to Jesus, I believed that Jesus was the truth. That meant that everything He said was true — even when it was quite a staggering idea.

One astonishing fact is that those who believe in Jesus will do mightier works than even He did. When Jesus made this statement, He prefixed it with the words, 'I tell you the truth.' It was as if He knew that people would question whether such a wonderful promise could be possible. Indeed, many believers today try to water it down. 'He was really referring to first-century Christians,' they declare. Or they suggest that His words should be interpreted to mean something other than what they say.

But Jesus wasn't talking specifically about the early church, but about people who have faith in Him regardless of when they live. And since the context is miracles, the most natural interpretation is that He was talking about our performing actual signs and wonders. Jesus is inviting us to believe Him and to bring in not just a Kingdom of words, but of power.

My children came with me to the crusade at Costa Rica. They saw hundreds being born again, healed and delivered and they said to

## ■ To encourage

Don't disqualify yourself — this is for everyone.

Jesus said 'anyone' who has faith.

The key is not who you are but what your faith is like. Keep praying for faith and take every opportunity to put it into action. The more experience you have of seeing God's power at work, the more your faith will grow.

## ■ To meditate on

We need faith.
'I tell you the truth, if you have faith as small as a mustard seed, you can say to this mountain, "Move from here to there" and it will move. Nothing will be impossible for you' (Matt. 17:20b).
'We live by faith, not by sight' (2 Cor. 5:7).

4 , 11 , 14   39

   43   44

—————————————

       (37)

me, 'Daddy, we want to do what you do.' I laid my hands on them and prayed, 'Lord, let them do far more than me.'

Isn't that the longing of any father for his children — that they do much more than he does? Jesus came to reveal the Father's heart for us and He doesn't say, 'I'll let you perform only some of My wonders — just so that you know who's boss.' He says, 'You go for it! I want to fulfil My plans through you and that includes your doing greater works than Me.'

Does Jesus promise that we will do these things because we're super people who have got all our theology right? No. He empowers us 'because I am going to the Father.' Jesus is no longer with us as a human being so we must carry on the miracles that He began. That's why He gave us His Holy Spirit — to enable us to be His witnesses in word and action.

Wherever you go, you will see situations that are full of darkness. Jesus is the Light of the World and we are His ambassadors. It's time for you to reach out in faith for 'greater things than these' that people 'may see your good [sometimes miraculous] deeds and praise your Father in heaven' (Matt. 5:16b).

## ■ Food for thought

➢ People often find that they have more faith in one area than another, e.g. faith for finance, faith for healing, etc.

➢ Make a list of your own experience of God's power. Do you have more experience in one particular area?

➢ This could be your launch pad into ministry. If it is in seeing people saved then start preaching the gospel, if healing start praying for the sick. As your faith grows in this area you can branch out into new ministries.

➢ Keep praying that the Lord will use you. Tell Him that you are willing to serve Him in this way.

## ■ To understand

You don't have to be a 'big name ministry' to have the opportunity to see God's power in action.

God has created each one of us 'to do good works which (he) prepared in advance for us to do' (Eph. 2:10).

Wherever you are, the Lord has a ministry for you. Keep in tune with Him and He will lead you in your everyday life into situations where you can do greater works. If you are always waiting for a platform you will miss out and so will the people around you who need help.

**Praise God, it is our destiny to win. It is our destiny to be victorious with Christ Jesus. It is our destiny to receive the fullness of the kingdom of God — but only if we're willing and prepared to take what is rightfully ours from the clutches of the enemy. I challenge you today: Be God's warrior in this hour!**
*Larry Lea*

# Can these bones live?

The hand of the LORD was upon me, and he brought me out by the Spirit of the LORD and set me in the middle of a valley; it was full of bones. He led me to and fro among them, and I saw a great many bones on the floor of the valley, bones that were very dry. He asked me, 'Son of man, can these bones live?' I said, 'O Sovereign LORD, you alone know' (Ezek. 37:1–3).

'Everything is possible for him who believes' (Mark 9:23b).

T he hand of the Lord was upon Ezekiel. God's people demonstrate that His hand is on them when they put Jesus first. They know that His hand is a hand of mercy and love so they don't try to shrug it off when it's pointing them in a difficult direction. They allow God to lead them wherever He wants them to go.

Ezekiel wasn't set down on a mountain top amid the glory of God; he was put in a valley of dry bones. When that happens, you begin wondering if the hand of the Lord really is on you. God places you in a hard situation and all you see are dry bones. Your housegroup isn't getting anywhere, or your colleagues at work show no interest in the gospel, or you haven't been healed, or your family are hostile because you believe in Jesus. Society itself speaks to you of dryness and death. You open your newspaper and see violence, child abuse, addictions, divorce and abortion, and you pant for streams of revival in the desert.

'Can these bones live?' God asked Ezekiel. I once ministered to a vast number of Hindus and Moslems. If God had asked me this question before that crusade, I'd probably have replied, 'I don't think so, Lord. They're idol

■ **To analyse**

Are you in a valley?

Have you become dry?

Consider whether or not you have been moving in the power of the Spirit or living out of your own strength.

■ **To meditate on**

The importance of living by faith. 'Now faith is being sure of what we hope for and certain of what we do not see' (Heb. 11:1). 'And without faith it is impossible to please God, because anyone who comes to him must believe that he exists and that he rewards those who earnestly seek him' (Heb. 11:6).

worshippers. Look at their huge ornate temples and mosques. There are demons everywhere! I doubt that these bones can live.' But I proclaimed Christ and ten thousand of them were saved.

When Ezekiel answered God, he said, 'Lord, you alone know.' That's the statement of faith that God wants to hear from us all. When we turn to Him with this reply, we're affirming that He's our only source of healing and deliverance.

For too long believers have fixed their eyes on themselves and not on God. Many of us have been doing things in our own strength and now we're exhausted and discouraged. The devil has stolen our joy and we're complaining, 'Why am I in this valley of dry bones?' But we're not there by accident. The opposition may be attacking furiously, but there will come a day when God will prepare a table in the presence of our enemies and breakthrough will come.

We must shake off unbelief. God doesn't want to lead a group of cowards who whimper, 'I'm going to let my little light shine.' He wants to raise up an army of men and women who have great vision and faith, who do great things and who give Him great glory.

➢ Read Psalm 23. 'Even though I walk through the valley of the shadow of death ...'

➢ In a notebook paraphrase the first four verses. What does it mean for God to be our shepherd, make us lie down in green pastures, etc.? Give modern everyday examples of how He does these things. If you're feeling dry ask Him to refresh and restore you.

### ■ To confess

Are there any situations confronting you where you feel there is no hope?

Confess to the Lord what you are feeling.

Reaffirm your faith in His purposes for you.

It does not matter how long you have been in the Christian life, you are dependent upon Him for every step. Without Him we can do nothing. We can only conquer our doubts by looking steadily at Him and by not looking at them. The way to answer them is to look at Him. The more you know Him and His glory the more ridiculous they will become.
*Martyn Lloyd-Jones*

# Prophesy to these bones

'Prophesy to these bones and say to them, ... "This is what the Sovereign LORD says to these bones: ... I will put breath in you, and you will come to life."' ... So I prophesied as I was commanded. And as I was prophesying, there was a noise, a rattling sound, and the bones came together, bone to bone. I looked, and tendons and flesh appeared on them and skin covered them, but there was no breath in them. Then he said to me, 'Prophesy to the breath; ... and say to it ... "Come from the four winds, O breath, and breathe into these slain, that they may live."' So I prophesied as he commanded me, and breath entered them; they came to life and stood up on their feet — a vast army (Ezek. 37:4–10).

G od told Ezekiel to prophesy, 'Dry bones, hear the word of the Lord!' Modern society is brainwashed by people's opinions. You only have to turn on your TV to find people locked in debate over some topical issue. Into this melée of different viewpoints speaks the most important voice of all — the Word of God.

Ezekiel could easily have questioned the apparent stupidity of what he was being told to do. But he was wise enough to realise that God knew what He was talking about and followed the command to the letter. That's always the secret of success: complete obedience to the Word of God. I believe that God wants to pour out on us a mighty blessing, but He's looking for Ezekiels — obedient men and women — to play a vital part in it.

Immediately Ezekiel prophesied, there was a rattling noise. Whenever God starts doing something extraordinary there's a shaking. Someone faithfully speaks the living Word, the people receive it and it devastates them. At that crusade I mentioned I called on the Hindus and Moslems to renounce Krishna and Mohammed. As they did so, a wave of the Spirit swept through the crowd and several hundred fell to

## ■ To question

What has the Lord told you to do?

_____

Have you completely obeyed Him in this?

Are you completely obeying the Word of God revealed in the Bible?

## ■ To meditate on

The Spirit comes at God's command. 'I will pour out my Spirit on all people ... Even on my servants, both men and women, I will pour out my Spirit in those days' (Joel 2:28,29).
'And with that he breathed on them and said, "Receive the Holy Spirit"' (John 20:22).

the ground. Demons surfaced, screamed and came out. There was a rattling.

Ezekiel didn't have to sit and work out which bone went where! God fitted them together and put flesh on them. In times of restoration He builds up the body of Christ and gives particular gifts on each individual member.

When Ezekiel prophesied to the breath, the people stood up and resembled a mighty army. Unbelievers may ridicule and malign the church. They may think, 'It's a load of dry bones.' But God is bringing together and raising up a great company of people who will conquer the nations for His Son..You may look at your life and question, 'How could He possibly use a dry bone like me?' But you're included in God's army and it's your destiny to tear down strongholds for Jesus.

We're living at a glorious time. God's Spirit is being poured out on men, women and even children. God is refreshing and empowering us as never before. And He's sending us into the valley of dry bones — the place of death. What do we do there? We speak the Word of life and we watch as God performs awesome wonders and brings multitudes into the Kingdom.

## ■ Food for thought

➤ 'For the earth *will* be full of the knowledge of the LORD as the waters cover the sea' (Isa. 11:9b – editor's italics).

➤ This prophecy gives us faith to pray for our nations and the world. Set aside some time this week to pray for revival. Ask God for an outpouring of His Spirit such as we have never seen before.

➤ Why not fast when you pray?

## ■ To encourage

The Bible exhorts us to encourage one another.

One very practical way in which we can do this is to speak the living Word to one another.

Over the next week make it your aim to encourage others in this way.

It could well be that you will prophesy to another's dry bones.

Do you believe in revival, my friend? Are you praying for revival? What are you trusting? Are you trusting the organizing power of the church? Or are you trusting in the power of God to pour out his Spirit upon us again, to revive us, to baptize us anew and afresh with his most blessed Holy Spirit?
*Martyn Lloyd-Jones*

# The gospel of the kingdom

'And this gospel of the kingdom will be preached in the whole world as a testimony to all nations, and then the end will come' (Matt. 24:14).

As I've already said, I believe that we're living in very exciting times. This age is coming to a great climax. All around us there's an outpouring of violence and filth, but we're going to see the most wonderful things happening in the church before Christ returns.

Jesus preached 'the gospel of the kingdom'. It comprised words and wonders. The early disciples remembered what Jesus had said to them: 'As the Father has sent me, I am sending you' (John 20:21b). They declared the same gospel and witnessed the same signs.

God wants His people to stop serving empty theology and tradition and to begin moving in love and power. We have a relationship with the person who miraculously created the world out of nothing. So how can we say that something is too hard for Him?

When I was at a crusade in Lagos I preached and then invited the crippled, blind, deaf and dumb to come up for prayer. The first one was a girl of nine who had been born blind. I put my hands on her, prayed and saw God restore her sight. Two dozen reporters interviewed me about this miracle. 'Here's her address,' I told them. 'You check it out.' The following morning

## ■ To realise

Has your witness to the gospel been in word only?

Of course it is good to share the gospel but what a powerful proof of the existence of God is the demonstration of His power!

Adjust your thinking, expect signs and wonders to follow your preaching of the Word. Pray for it and believe that God will answer you.

## ■ To meditate on

Signs should accompany preaching. 'Now, Lord ... enable your servants to speak your word with great boldness. Stretch out your hand to heal and perform miraculous signs and wonders through the name of your holy servant Jesus' (Acts 4:29,30).
'Our gospel came to you not simply with words, but also with power, with the Holy Spirit and deep conviction' (1 Thess. 1:5).

the story was on the front page of most of the Lagos newspapers. That's the impact you have when you preach the gospel of the Kingdom.

Wherever we go, we take the Kingdom with us and no demonic power can stand in our presence. I discovered this when I was working at the school for mentally handicapped children. The devil prompted all kinds of filthy behaviour among those kids but I would pray, 'Lord, I'm bringing the Kingdom into this.' The staff were amazed at what happened. They told me that normally the children would be screaming and fighting one another but that when I was present, there was an unusual calm. So don't allow the devil to play games with you. Take authority wherever you are.

In the past few years I've seen Jesus perform all the healing miracles that He did in the Gospels. He's using me in this ministry, but I long to see signs and wonders multiplied throughout the church. God is looking for men and women who model their lives on His Son; people who don't preach half a gospel but who have faith to do the powerful works of the Kingdom; people who are prepared to give every ounce of energy to glorify His name.

## ■ Food for thought

➤ What specific things has God said to you through these studies? Are you obeying what He has said? If not, ask Him to help you obey.

➤ Consider the parts of the study material you may have skipped over. Does God want to speak to you through those? Do you believe that His promises are for you? Are you moving in faith?

➤ Anyone who has faith in Jesus will do greater works than He did. Then we will see the gospel of the Kingdom reaping a harvest of multitudes.

## ■ To identify

Identify Christians you know who are doing the works of the Kingdom. Ask them if they will pray for you and lay hands on you.

Arrange to pray with them regularly; let their faith rub off on you.

Accompany them as they pray for people and simply begin to move out in faith yourself.

The expansion of the ministry of signs and wonders from the One to many has cosmic effects ... The expansion of the kingdom of God – and accompanying defeat of Satan – is effected by the number of Christians performing signs and wonders.
*John Wimber*

# Thick darkness

'See, darkness covers the earth and thick darkness is over the peoples' (Isa. 60:2a).

W e're living in an age of thick darkness. I meet it in Africa where there are hundreds of sorcerers who are moving in the most uncanny supernatural realms. Some of the stories about them would make your hair stand on end. They can supposedly change form at night and do the strangest things. We have video testimony of a sorcerer confessing to eating human flesh.

In Africa it's relatively easy to see the difference between darkness and light because the sins of the people are so obvious — even to unbelievers. But when we consider our own western civilisation, we tend to view it differently. Our society doesn't deal in darkness and light but in shades of grey. We're educated to think in terms of compromise and if anyone dares to suggest that 'This is wrong and that's right' he's considered bigoted.

But the fact is that sin in the western world is just as heinous as it is in the darkest corner of Africa. Daily we witness rebellion and bloodshed in our major cities and are haunted by the pictures of the dead being carried off in body bags. We see the angry grieving families, the armed gangs, the wounded children and the burned-out cars. We hear about the drug

## ■ Be prepared

When issues of righteousness and justice are raised or debated make sure a Christian voice is heard by writing to your MP or local newspaper.

## ■ To meditate on

This is the verdict.
'Light has come into the world, but men loved darkness instead of light because their deeds were evil. Everyone who does evil hates the light ... for fear that his deeds will be exposed. But whoever lives by the truth comes into the light, so that it may be seen plainly that what he has done has been done through God'
(John 3:19–21).

dealers shooting it out on street corners and learn that the Mafia is making billions of dollars a year through its two hundred child pornography magazines.

I look at the darkness in Africa and recoil at the idea of eating human flesh, but I notice that although the people there are malnourished, they love their babies. In the western world we have an abundance of almost everything but we casually destroy little babies before they get the chance to breathe. In 1968 there were 25,000 abortions in England, Wales and Scotland and by 1989 this figure had risen to 194,000. One in four conceptions in Britain ends in abortion.

Thick darkness is over the peoples and God wants to come in and meet their desperate needs. I often pray, 'Lord, if You're doing anything on earth, I want to be right at the centre of it. I don't want to miss out on what You're doing. I want to be where You're saving, healing and delivering.' Jesus said, 'Whoever serves me must follow me; and where I am, my servant also will be' (John 12:26a). If you're His disciple you won't be frittering away your life on incidentals. You'll be right there with Him, keen to serve Him in any way you can.

## ■ To beware

As the day fades into dusk our eyes adjust and we are hardly conscious of the night drawing in until a light is turned on.

What areas of darkness in your land have you simply grown used to?

... if society deteriorates and its standards decline, till it becomes like a dark night or stinking fish, there is no sense in blaming society, for that is what happens when fallen men and women are left to themselves and human selfishness is unchecked. The question to ask is 'Where is the church? Why are the salt and light of Jesus Christ not permeating and changing our society?'
*John Stott*

# Arise, shine

'Arise, shine, for your light has come, and the glory of the LORD rises upon you ... Nations will come to your light, and kings to the brightness of your dawn' (Isa. 60:1,3).

'There will be a time of distress such as has not happened from the beginning of nations until then. But at that time your people — everyone whose name is found written in the book — will be delivered. Multitudes who sleep in the dust of the earth will awake: some to everlasting life, others to shame and everlasting contempt. Those who are wise will shine like the brightness of the heavens, and those who lead many to righteousness, like the stars for ever and ever' (Dan. 12:1-3).

W e live in the midst of darkness. On the one hand we can't ignore that and try to hide, but neither must we be overwhelmed by the terrible things that are happening around us. God wants us to focus on Jesus, the light. The world's darkness is our cue to shine.

When Solomon dedicated the temple, the glory of the Lord filled it (2 Chr. 7:1). Believers are now God's temple and at Pentecost, God poured out His Holy Spirit on them (Acts 2: 1–4). When the Spirit comes, the presence and glory of the Lord are upon His people. In the midst of the darkness God wants His anointing to rest upon us as never before.

God told Daniel that in the end times there would be unparalleled distress on the earth, but that His people would be delivered. He said that in those days the wise would shine. They aren't the ones who live to make money or gain knowledge. Certainly God wants to channel the wealth of the wicked into the hands of the righteous, but the wise are those who win souls (Prov. 11:30b). And they will shine like the stars for ever. When do stars shine? In the darkness.

The anointing of God rests upon us so that we can shine for His glory. I didn't begin my

## ■ To analyse

Jesus warns against hiding our light under a bowl (Matt. 5:15) where it is of no use to anyone.

Are there any situations in your life where you cover up the light within you?

## ■ To meditate on

Let your light shine!
'Let your light shine before men, that they may see your good deeds and praise your Father in heaven' (Matt. 5:16b)
'For God, who said, "Let light shine out of darkness," made his light shine in our hearts to give us the light of the knowledge of the glory of God in the face of Christ' (2 Cor. 4:6).